DEDICATION

This book is dedicated to my Mum and Dad. Thank you for your love and belief in me and all my friends and family for being a part of my journey. Lastly, to three incredible Life and Empowerment Coaches who were there when I was ready. Bless you all xx

.

A Personal Message from Claire

Believe in yourself
and anything is possible.
Happy reading.

GIGIbE
WITh LOVE

X

Claire thank you so much for
your frendship support and love
every blessing in your new
job

Lots of love
Claire H

IT'S MY TURN NOW

A Journey Towards Freedom

CLAIRE BLOOMFIELD

Disclaimer

This book is designed to provide information and motivation to our readers. It is sold with the understanding that the author and publisher are not engaged to render any type of psychological, legal, or any other kind of professional advice. The content is the sole expression and opinion of its author. Neither the publisher nor the individual author(s) shall be liable for any physical, psychological, emotional, financial, or commercial damages, including, but not limited to, special, incidental, consequential or other damages. Our views and rights are the same: You are responsible for your own choices, actions, and results.

The content of the book is solely written by the author.

DVG STAR Publishing is not liable for the content of the book.

Published by DVG STAR PUBLISHING

www.dvgstar.com

email us at info@dvgstar.com

NO PART OF THIS WORK MAY BE REPRODUCED OR STORED IN AN INFORMATIONAL RETRIEVAL SYSTEM, WITHOUT THE EXPRESS PERMISSION OF THE PUBLISHER IN WRITING.

Contents

PROLOGUE

Write a book?? Who me? Never!! That was my reaction when I was asked to write a book on my life journey. I'm an ordinary woman living an ordinary life. There is nothing remarkable about me at all. I'm living the life I've been given.

As you read this book, you could be forgiven for thinking that too, and you'd be right. Why would I write a book? That is a good question.

We are all on a journey in life, whether we realise it or not - this book is my journey. There have been many obstacles placed in my path, some of which have been removed. Some of which remain. You may connect with my story on some level; it may strike a chord with you.

It is my sincere prayer that whatever your situation, you realise that nothing is impossible, there are always solutions. Lastly, never give up on either your Dreams or this Adventure called Life.

Thank you for taking the time to read my story.

FOREWORD

I am so grateful to be invited to write the foreword of this book for Claire Bloomfield. This autobiography of Claire's life is a real inspirational book that's best introduced via a story of how I met Claire.

This story will give you an idea of the character of whom Claire is and why the book has been aptly titled, "It's My Turn Now!"

To give you some context around this story, I am about to share with you my story. This is a story I often share with my delegates and students to inspire them to make tough decisions. I hope the story of me meeting Claire and her friend Karen inspires you to take action on what you want to do.

Here's the story as I normally deliver it…Enjoy:

Have you ever had a difficult decision to make?

If you've ever had a difficult decision to make? Just nod your head if you've had to make a difficult decision in the past!

Not only did you have a difficult decision to make, but also, this decision had a 50/50 chance of either going right or going wrong – and it will hinder or even jeopardize your credibility. It could also affect your income earning capacity.

If you were with me on Friday evening in Norwich, my partner and I were sat in our living room, on a big brown leather three seater sofa. You would have witnessed the conversation she was having on the telephone. She was speaking on the phone to a guy called Steve.

Steve is one of those guys who is very excitable, with loads of energy, Steve was the current chairperson for the Yes Group Essex.

Have you heard of the 'Yes Group'? Raise your hand if you've heard about the 'Yes Group'? For those of you that have never heard of the 'Yes Group', It is a personal development group of like-minded people who meet once a month to share, learn, grow and contribute, like our PSA (Professional Speaker's Academy) family.

The 'Yes Group Essex Leadership' team had just commissioned my company (Think! Training & Consultancy) to do a dynamic event for them – and the conversation went like this…

Louise, by the way, had short dark hair at the time; she's got quite the babyface. She's one of those ladies that loves to make things happen and she's very driven.

She was having this conversation with Steve; she said

"Steve, how many people have registered for this event?" Steve said.

"About 38!" They ended up with 70 plus delegates at the event. Louise said, "Okay! Are you looking forward to the event?"

Steve said, *"Yes, I'm really excited about it."*

And then he posed a question… And I'm sitting there unable to figure out what the question was about but I heard Louise say back:

"Hold on, hold on there, Steve, you can't decide that, that decision has to be decided by Tosin. He's the guy who's running the event."

And I'm wondering: 'What is she talking about?'

She said, *"Hold on a minute, let me pose the question to Tosin."*

She put the phone down and she turned around to me and said,

"At this event we have two women with disabilities, they would both like to come and do the event. I don't feel it's possible for them to do the event, what do you think?"

I pondered to myself for a while… And then I thought, you know what, I cannot decide whether they can or cannot do the event. I need to see them and assess what the disability is first and assess if they truly want to do the event themselves. Not just because they've raised money for charity and have now been cajoled into doing something that could potentially be very dangerous for them.

Let's fast forward to the event, we got to the venue which I drove down to from Norwich on a Sunday morning. It was such a beautiful drive because the night before it had rained and cleared all the snowfall from the previous week. Wow! It was so exciting, especially because as I was driving, you could see clear blue skies. It was so fresh it felt like the first day of spring. I could smell the fresh air, the grass and trees all looked new (beautiful lush green colours) because the rain had washed away all of the dirt.

We arrived at Orsett Hall in Essex which is a luxurious hotel, built on 12 acres of beautifully landscaped gardens. Beautiful scenery, beautiful decors and very friendly staff as well.

Now we were in a room similar to this one but it could hold about 150 people. It was called the White Hall Suite. We had 70 plus people register for the dynamic event in the end.

We had many activities going on in the room. Some people were setting up the audio and sound systems whilst I was organising myself preparing for the day ahead. The registration ladies were registering delegates as they were walking in. Suddenly, from the corner of my eye, I saw these two beautiful women with disabilities walking in.

There was Karen with her crutches and her feet spread wide apart in an awkward position. Long dark hair, very stockily built lady, who was kind of strong with a stern look on her face. She walked forwards, mimicking the walk of a penguin, just to keep herself upright.

And then, there was Claire, beautiful bright face, short blond bobbed hair with one of those funky looking strollers that she was grabbing on to with both hands (like holding tight to a steering wheel with both hands as you drive). Her feet were also in an awkward position. She was pushing along with the stroller to keep herself mobile and upright.

As I stood there and watched these ladies coming in through the corner of my eyes, I had a conversation with myself…

"Tosin, there is no way in hell that these ladies are going to walk!!!"

Due to the dynamic activity that we were commissioned to do, these ladies were about to do a FIREWALK. Measuring anything between 500 degrees Fahrenheit to 2500 degrees Fahrenheit. However, your average oven, ladies and gentlemen, is 250 degrees at its highest temperature which you can't even touch when it's that hot. SO, I HAD A TOUGH DECISION

TO MAKE!

So, we went out to light the fire, which we usually have a pit lane laid out (that's firewood laid in a circular fashion about 4 or 5 feet high which we set on fire). I connected the participants with the fire and instructed them on how the fire-walk session would run, then I got them all back into the fire-walk training room.

Now, as we were heading back to the room for the training, Karen and Claire were lagging behind for obvious reasons. So, I decided to have a conversation with the ladies:

First of all, I went to Karen and said,

"Karen, I understand you want to do the fire-walk?"

She looked straight into my eyes and said,

"Yes, Tosin, I want to do the fire-walk!"

I responded with,

"Okay Karen, I'll see what I can do…"

I moved on and ran across to meet Claire – I exaggerated there, I mean, I didn't exactly run across as she didn't get that far with her stroller?

I said, *"Claire, I understand you want to do the fire-walk?"*

She turned her head towards me and looked directly at me and said in a very sad voice,

"Tosin, you have no idea, I want this…I want to do the fire-walk. If anyone tells me that I can't… you have no idea what that would mean!"

I stood back up and straightened myself, and said, *"Wow! Claire, you're doing the fire-walk."*

She said, *"Really? Ahh! Thank you, thank you, thank you!"*

So, back in the training room what typically happens here is, I support the delegates to manage their own state. You need to be in an uptime state, not a downtime state to do a fire-walk. I was really energised, pumped up and working the audience with loud music to get them into a peak state for fire-walking.

On one hand, you had the Miss Universe Essex Girls too cool for school, looking pretty (swaying from side to side pretending to be dancing but more worried about how looked and if anyone was looking at them). So, they were all controlled, they didn't want to let loose and enjoy themselves because people might be watching them - Do you know people like this?

However, on the other hand, the music was playing and pumping where you had Claire with her stroller getting jiggy with the beats (I believe it was *'Snap – I've Got the Power'* playing at the time). She definitely had the power!!!

I stood there just blown away and I said to myself, *"Tosin, they're doing it. Claire and Karen are doing the fire-walk."*

Now it was time for the fire-walk – I normally walk first, then I come back and guide the rest of the delegates through. There I was guiding people through it... Go, go, go, go, go, go, go, go, go, go... until everybody had gone.

Now it was time for Karen and Claire's turn to walk. I went over to Karen and said,

"Are you ready?"

She said, *"Yes!"*

She took off her shoe's and stood in her awkward stance with one crutch on her right arm so I grabbed her left arm into an arm lock with mine.

"Karen, when I say, go, we go, are you ready?"

She said, *"Yes!"*

"Go!!!"

We both trooped across the hot embers of coal. I got her across and everyone was screaming and cheering for Karen. She took one of her crutches and put it in the air, shouting

"Yeah! Yes, Yes, YES".

She celebrated like crazy.

Now it was Claire's turn. I got over there, grabbed Claire and said,

"I need some assistance here, please", so I called,

"Steve over here, please?"

Steve ran across to help me out. He grabbed one hand and I grabbed the other hand. Someone else assisted her with her shoes. I also asked that someone take her stroller and shoes to the end of the fire-walk lane.

They took it over and I remember vividly grabbing her arm and she was bloody heavy.

Steve and I grabbed each arm, then I looked at Claire and said,

"Claire, are you ready?"
She said, *"Yes, I am ready Tosin."*
"When I say go, we all go together… Go!!!"

Steve and I carried her across by dipping her feet on the hot embers of coals intermittently as we carried her across. As we reached the end of the fire-walk lane, Claire said,

"That was absolutely amazing!"

She celebrated hysterically, you wouldn't have known she just walked on fire.

Now, here's the thing, Claire and Karen were prepared to do whatever it took to walk across the fire-walk. Are you prepared to do whatever it takes to become a world-class human being or a world-class speaker or a world-class Trainer and Coach or a world-class (Blank) you fill in the blank? If you say, yes you are, then all you have to do is make a decision today: to commit to that…whatever that is for you? That is all you have to do - make a decision one way or the other.

Claire and Karen decided they were walking on fire before they got there. Here's the thing, you haven't got any problems in your life but you'll have tough decisions to make instead Losers take all the time in the world to make them and keep changing their minds – Winners make them quickly and never doubt themselves. The real question is, which one are you?

If you want to become a world-class (Blank), then the speed of decision making and implementation will be the key to your success. Just make the decision; either way you will learn something—the end of the story.

So, in summary: It's definitely your turn now Claire and also you, the reader of this book. It's your turn now too. So, seize the moment and do something that you've always wanted to do. It's time to make that tough decision you've been putting off for a very long time.

I wish you an enriching journey of learning, growing and evolving through reading the book, **"It's My Turn Now - A journey towards freedom"**.

Tosin Ogunnusi (Author of "Time To Break Free!")

TESTIMONIAL FROM
CLAIRE'S COACH

Claire's story is set to be a best seller and will touch the minds and hearts of many.

I feel privileged to have supported Claire's personal growth and to have witnessed the moment when she realised she held the power inside of her to create the positive change she yearned for and had done so all along! This lightning moment, I will carry with me forever.

What Claire has accomplished professionally and in her personal development since that time has been exceptional. When I think of Claire and her gifts, this quote comes to mind.

"Some people wish it would happen; some want it to happen; others make it happen."

Claire truly does make it happen, her positive energy is infectious, and one thing I know for sure, it really is her turn now.

Lorna ~ Next Level Success Hypnotherapist and Mindset Coach

'If you don't know it's dark, you won't put the light on.'

Claire Bloomfield

Chapter One

INTRODUCTION

The whole idea of writing a book was such a foreign concept to me; I felt as though I wouldn't be able to collect my thoughts. I couldn't imagine all that work, but many people told me that I had made a lot of progress; that I made it encouraging for other people. I felt as though my life was quite ordinary, and people would not be interested; however, I understand how other people can view it as out of the ordinary.

Hence, I left it and left it and then there was my friend Alex; she actually runs a chiropractic clinic in Chelmsford; she put on Facebook that she had now qualified as an NLP coach. I was at a stage that I wasn't actually unhappily stuck; I felt I was stationary and not actually moving forward or going backwards. I was literally just stationary, so I said to her

"Do you just do corporate clients, or do you do paid clients, like individuals".

She explained that she only does corporate clients, and she advised,

"What I would do is put you in touch with Lorna, a lady that I know you will get along well with. Do you want me to introduce you to her?".

So I said, *"Yes, I would like you to do that",* and so she introduced us, and I said to Lorna,

"I don't actually know why I'm speaking to you. I'm not against speaking to you but I actually don't know why we actually came into contact and I'm not sure what I'm looking for because I'm not actually unhappy

about my life", so she said,

"*What about your career?*"

I explained that I didn't actually have a career because I gave up work over six years ago when my dad died suddenly. I worked for social services as an admin assistant. At first, I was a telephonist. I was only there initially for six weeks. However, it turned into twelve years on the job!! A real blessing!! I really enjoyed myself. I had been unemployed long-term, so after about four and a half weeks, I spoke to the union representative Jackie and explained that I couldn't go back to being unemployed as it was just something that I didn't think I could cope with. So she said to leave the situation with her and she managed to find me a contract to stay, which was so special to me. I worked on the switchboard for quite some time and then it was decided that it would be taken out to be centralised. So, I wondered about my job again, happily however, Pauline, the lady in charge of a section came over to us in the office and said it was not my fault that they were taking the switchboard away. It was their responsibility to find us other work. Consequently, I then learnt how to operate the computer and was able to do data entry and write letters. After some time, I was able to be put out on the reception and deal with customers face-to-face. So from a six-week work experience I gained a great deal and made some very special friends in the process.

After my dad had died, I felt as though I had to take time out during that time and reflect and smell the roses because it was a right shock to me and I actually haven't gone back to work since. I laughed and said things had changed, so I haven't gone back to work or found anything I wanted to do. I'm not unhappy about that because I'm doing stuff like going to the gym and going out most of the time with my friends. So, she said to me,

"*I sense that you are looking for your purpose.*"

so I said,

"*Yes, I suppose I am; all I know is that I want to help people.*"

and basically, she said,

"I feel like you want a job to do at the NLP."
I said, *"Yes, I would fancy that"*.
She carried on to say,
"I see you writing a book."
So I thought, no, don't start that again, don't start saying that to me because I can't deal with it right now. She went on to say,
"Why don't you see whether there are any online NLP courses."

Neuro-Linguistic Programming (NLP) is the art of lining up our internal thoughts and external words to synchronise with our external experience.

I knew a gentleman called Tosin, who was an NLP coach, so I called him up. Still, the thing is that I have never seen him online before, he's probably normally on online calls enough, I couldn't ring him up and ask him how he was; I would have to ring him up for a purpose. So I thought I'll ring him up because I want to know what the procedure was and things like that, so I phoned him. He said yes, he does do the NLP and he gave me the details. So, I found myself booked onto the course all done in one afternoon.

During the training, quite early on, he said,

"It would be a good idea if you could write a book because you'll be able to reach more people with it. For starters, your influence will be wider, if you're going to be doing self-development as you would be more inclined to get more clients by becoming an author. Especially with the life experiences you have, it's all about leverage and how it connects you with another person and that's exactly what I do".

That sounded so fascinating to me and it felt at that point that it was time for me; to share my story with the world. It was now my turn to be in the so-called "**spotlight**".

Therefore, it wasn't actually my idea, so I still get surprised by the idea that someone will be interested in my book. My true connection is to share my story, which will allow me to connect with you as a reader. You may have gone through the same journey as me, or you may get inspired by the journey I've been on and how I've been able to change my life around. I'm hoping that this book will inspire you; you will learn from my journey that life is worth living and that whatever disability you may have or don't have, it won't stop you from achieving your dreams and goals.

I've always felt that everyone else had got on the bandwagon before me. Everybody else had done things that they had wanted to do, like going to drama school or had their dreams fulfilled. It's not like I haven't had my dreams come true because there are dreams that have happened for me so I'm not saying that I haven't had anything good. However, the carousel has come around to me now and now the spotlight has given me the chance to shine and show people what I have achieved.

Although, I have still had dreams that haven't happened to me; for example, I always wanted to go to drama school and be an actress on stage. The part that stopped me was the fact that I didn't believe I could have ever got there. To be fair, I would have believed that my physical disability would have stopped me because in my mind, at that time, I didn't feel the same as I did now. I wasn't confident in my own abilities. It was always for somebody else to do it; it always felt like it was somebody else's limelight but now I'm ready to share my story. I was my own limiting factor. It has been my mind along the whole journey from an early age.

The dictionary defines hope as 'a certain thing to happen, a feeling of anticipation and desire.' An ideal is defined as 'fulfilling one's conception of what is best, most fitting.' In conclusion, it is fair to assume that you have an expectation and desire for what is most appropriate for yourself. Hope seems refreshingly spacious in comparison to faith. It is bigger and inclusive because it doesn't need acceptance of personal values, nor is it married to ideologies. Indeed, within religious traditions and beyond them, hope, while essential for our well-being, can exist with equal intensity.

Hope, since it is universal, is convincing. All human borders are crossed: age, colour, class, gender, ethnicity, faith, politics or any other persuasion. Everyone wants it and if they have made it as far as this day, almost everyone displays at least some amount of hope.

But it is not enough to only *'wish'* that anything could happen. Hope is important because hope requires the ability to get there and multiple paths for you to follow. Life can be hard but that shouldn't come as a surprise to anyone. Yet, optimism helps you to continue to go down new paths, see different things and strive to make something your perfect ideal. This holds true even though there does not seem to be a solution. In fact, in the meaning of the word *'faith'* the word *'hope'* is confidence, the essence of things wished for, the confirmation of things that have not been shown. Besides, confidence without deeds is dead. In other words, if you want something to happen but you don't do anything to work for it, then it's pointless. We have to take steps for our hope in order for us to fulfil our ideal of hope.

It is easiest to have faith in your life when things are going well. It's when life becomes rough that we need to use hope the most.

Now to let you into the world
of Claire Bloomfield,
of how it all began…….

The Canary

There was a Canary
Who lived in a cage
He was Green and Yellow
Rather small for his age

The Canary was used to life in his cage
That was his world
Without thought of rage

One day the cage door was opened a chink
The Canary was excited
He didn't know what to think
For so long confined to the inside of a cage
There were now possibilities –
He wanted to engage
Hesitantly, he hopped to the door
And pushed with his beak –
It had never opened before
The Canary just looked for a few minutes more
Then tentatively hopped just outside the cage door

The sky was blue
There was no hint of a cloud
Surely, this much fun was never allowed
Eventually the Canary decided to fly
There was just too much temptation
Up there in the sky
All the Canary knew was that being
Stuck on the ground
Was keeping the anxiety he had all around

So he decided to fly –
Cautiously at first
Suddenly he was so happy
He thought he would burst
From his vantage point
Way up in the blue
There was such a
Marvellous, Magnificent view
Nothing had changed –
Fundamentally that's true
But up in the sky
His perspective was new
He was still a Canary –
That was for sure
But he imagined being an eagle
So now he could soar!
Way above the issues and problems he knew
Seeing life through an eagle's eyes
Completely altered his view
Now with his vision enlarged
And a Song in his heart
The Canary firmly believed
He could make a new start

Claire Bloomfield (January 2008)

The Diamond

Once there was a Diamond called Dusty
Hidden in the Ground
It lay dirty and forgotten
Totally alone
Apparently by worth and circumstances bound

Suddenly there was a commotion
Right above where Dusty lay
Poor Dusty Didn't understand
What on earth was happening today?

The ground shifted around her
Dusty felt suddenly sick
She felt herself being lifted out of the ground
By a mechanical shovel or pick

Wait though – The shovel is not mechanical
It's held by a gentle firm hand
Suddenly Dusty hears a voice Say
"This Diamond's exquisite
When it is cleaned and polished
It will be quite Grand

Just like Dusty
We can lose sight of our value and worth
When the storms of life hit us
It's easy to lose focus
Wonder why and how
Certain circumstances
Came to birth

In Life we're not promised no trials
We are not promised no pain
But we're are promised
"This too shall pass"
"You will walk in Sunshine again"

This poem came out
Of a "Picture"
The briefest glimpse of a Diamond I Saw
God told me that people are Diamonds
In His eyes
You have not one flaw

You are special and unique
You have the gift of encouragement
That people seek
Your Diamond is buried
Down deep within
To give it away
Is where to begin

Look below the surface and
You will see
Your gift of a Diamond
You've given to me

Claire Bloomfield (March 2009)

'The Light can overcome the darkness, but the Darkness will never overcome the light'

Chapter Two

THE BIRTH

The Emergence Of Claire Bloomfield

When I was born, I didn't realise I was on a journey – I don't know what I thought, but I know that I wouldn't have understood the magnitude of the ride or, at times, how soul searching and how difficult it would prove to be. I'm thankful to have always had the support and love of family and friends and a deep spiritual awareness from an early age which I value.

Perhaps now I should mention that I was born prematurely, which resulted in me having Cerebral Palsy, which means that my balance and coordination are affected. My disability was not discovered until I was eighteen months old and only then because I wasn't walking.

Cerebral Palsy (CP) is the name given to a group of lifelong conditions that influence movement and coordination. It is triggered by a brain problem that develops before, during, or soon after birth. CP is not one condition only. It's a continuum of motion disorders that manifest in symptoms that differ from child to child.

Talking about my birth, my Mum told me that she thought my disability was due to an injection given as a child but I don't

It. It was the 10th of May 1962 when I embarked on my ...ney. It was a very memorable day for me; my birthday. I was supposed to be born at the beginning of July, so I was a couple of months premature, roughly seven weeks. I've always thought that may have been the result of my disability rather than the injection that my Mum referred to. Even though my Mum believed that it was the injection that caused it when I was young, I always felt better believing it was because I was born early, although now I have a phobia of needles and injections and anything to do with doctors and hospitals and that's because of all the operations I've had as a child

As I said, they didn't actually discover anything until I was eighteen months old because I was doing everything a baby my age would do. I was able to turn over, acknowledge people's faces and even crawl around. It wasn't until they noticed that I wasn't walking that they saw a difference. At the time, no one thought any different.

My Mum was quite protective, so people just thought I would start walking and we just had to give myself the time to develop as all babies walk at different times in their lives. Unfortunately, it just didn't happen for me. My Mum thought it was a side effect due to the rubella jab that caused it. I was seven weeks premature and the doctors didn't pick up on the symptoms. My Mum was a medical secretary at the time so it was very strange because they should have picked up on it earlier. They just thought she was an overprotective mother worrying about nothing as it were.

People with cerebral paralysis may have uncontrolled or spontaneous movements, muscles may be stiff, sluggish or rigid and people may have jerky motions or tremors in some cases. I used to get fits until I was 12 years of age but they used to say that if you lasted three years without them, you could say that they were gone. I always used to go for two years and not have one until the third year. They were always in the evenings. They said this might have been the case because the brain settles down at night and the electrical impulses start working. They were very rare but I used to take pills for it, a small dose of them to keep the fits under control and it managed to do just that most of the time. They practically went on throughout the night. But after that, I didn't have any more. The last time they were really bad but thankfully they have gone since then. The fits were the one thing that made me feel different from anyone else.

I think I got off quite lightly. Yes, I do have issues with my mobility but I can still get around; I go to the gym twice a week, so I thought nothing of it because I still get enjoyment by seeing my friends and so I have not been affected tremendously.

I didn't think that I was different from any other child in my childhood because I went to a nursery for able-bodied children. My friend also came because he also had a disability so I did not feel different from anyone else. I realised I was different from people but as a child, I had a very protective and supportive family. It didn't really impact me until I was older.

Sunday School

Nan was the Sunday school leader and used to go every Sunday with her to church. I enjoyed Sunday school and church as it built on what I was used to. My family including my Mum and Nan went, so the connection with them was strong. I learnt bible stories: such as the story of a man being lowered down into a roof. His friends brought him to Jesus and lowered him down through the roof. It taught me that anything was possible. It's all about self-belief and if I believe in myself, then things will happen for the better. It's all down to our mindset. Even somebody on a bed can be cured; even the blind man. I loved the stories and the parables, they were just a whole different realm of imagination and a world where anything was possible.

Brownies

I enjoyed Brownies on a Saturday afternoon. I was seven or

eight years old at the time. I remember going the first time away from Mum and Dad. I went on a week trip away from home. I managed it better than I thought I would. I looked after my friend and stayed and encouraged her. Mum used to write to me every day.

We also went on a day trip to Walton-on-the-Naze in Essex. I loved being included. There was a day when a wedding clashed with my Brownies so I told Mum and Dad that I didn't want to miss out on Brownies so they arranged for me to go home with Brown Owl until I was picked up from there as I didn't want to miss going to Brownies.

Horse Riding

I was seven years old when I started horse riding. I went from school every couple of weeks and never missed it. I also went to weekend lessons as well. After I finished school, I carried on doing weekend lessons. I loved it; it gave me the feeling that I could achieve anything if I put my mind to it. When I was on top of the horse, I felt as though I was on top of the world meaning I could lose the disability. The horse became my mobility. It became my legs. I used to have certain exercises that I used to have to do on the horse. Of course, I got side help to ensure that I didn't slide off. We'd do balance exercises and ride without stirrups. You experience everything. Your world just changes. Horses are very special animals because they have to be so patient with us – I thought it was great fun.

I particularly enjoyed the times when we could ride outside or go up the lane and over the bridge to the reserve. However, I wasn't too keen on going into the river.

Once during a Sunday morning lesson on a lovely day, we had gone into the river. Suddenly, from nowhere, my horse Honey Boy, had the idea that he wanted to trot. Needless to say, we took off at a rate of knots with the instructor yelling,

"Hold on, hold on."

I stayed on, but to this day, I don't know-how. I was more scared of falling in the river than staying on my horse.

Although it was scary, I remember being very proud of myself. When we went riding from school, the best rider gained house points as an incentive to improve (we belonged to houses at school).

Once Hadley, a bay horse that I was riding, started rearing intermittently during the lesson. Fortunately, I was able to grip very hard with my legs so that's exactly what I did – the more Hadley tried to dislodge me, the more I held on. He kept this up for two weeks until I couldn't ride him anymore. I rode until I was 21 years old and then stopped for 20 years. I have now been riding again for the last five or six years and love it. I have a good relationship with my horse Jake and I am much more confident.

Salvation Army Music School

During my childhood, I went to Salvation Army music school; I got involved with them. I went to music school there so I would have been about 17 years old. One of the leaders was a really good friend of mine, I used to use a wheelchair most of the time, and he said to me,

"Why are you just sitting there? You can get up and join!"

I thought, 'What on earth do you know about it?' You don't know how difficult this is, 'Why are you going on at me when you don't know anything about it?' I was resentful of him, he clearly didn't understand what was occurring but that only lasted about a year or so. Then I realised that he wasn't doing it to be a bully; he was just doing it to show me that I had to keep moving and I can't give into this. He did me a favour but at the time I thought, 'What on earth do you understand about this situation and you can't say that when you're walking around with no problems at all?' We got on very well once I understood him, after all, I needed someone like that to push me out of my comfort zone because no one else was telling me that I had it together or to just keep on going.

I probably wasn't taking a lot of the responsibility at the time, let's face it, I had a nice life as people were looking after me so I didn't have to take much responsibility when people were doing all that for me, so why would I bother.

Doug was his name, he was the type of person who was very straight up with people and spoke his mind. Down the line, he tried to say it with love. He wasn't being a bully; it was just how I saw it at the time. I felt as though he didn't understand but he actually understood me more than I realised. I saw people as not happy with me; that was sort of my defense mechanism. I don't resent my disability because it has given me more than it has taken away from me.

For example, if someone has a disability and could do things but can't now, I would sympathise. In contrast, I'm on the other end of the scale because my mind has changed but physically nothing has altered. As long as your mind changes, it doesn't matter; you can get through stuff physically. Sometimes nothing changes but you're nearly halfway there if the attitude changes. When you have a positive mindset, everything changes, so I decided that my disability is my power. I'm going to use it as a benefit to drive me forward and know that everything happens for a reason in life.

I Nearly Drowned When I Was 12 Years Old

This happened in the swimming pool during my school years. I used to go to lessons at the local swimming pool. The week before, my friend had taught me to swim with a ring and armbands, which made me feel pretty confident but she had told me that she wouldn't be here the following week.

As the day approached, I thought to myself, 'Okay, if I take a ring and armbands, I should be fine.' So, I get into the pool with all my gear and I'm really swimming. However, what I don't realise is that I'm going further and further towards the deep end.

There was no one in the pool at the time. I was quite close to the poolside; however, I didn't realise that the ring was letting the air out! The ring had a puncture! I didn't realise that I was floating more towards the deep end but by that time I realised I couldn't put my feet on the floor. So suddenly I was going under. I can remember my head going underwater and me trying to pull myself up but I couldn't. I just kept sinking like a brick. It is only because a lifeguard saw me that I'm alive today to tell the tale. I was so ill from doing that and swallowing all the chlorine. That instilled fear in me and I could not go near a swimming pool for a year or more after the event. I was petrified and I still am. Being near water brought back the feeling of drowning.

I figured that that trauma gave me a second chance to achieve more in life. The last time I went into the sea was at a beach in South Africa. My friend took his surfboard and he pulled me in. I got on it for literally all of five seconds.

The drowning experience instilled a phobia for swimming in me but nothing is permanent. We all need that push of faith to overcome the fear.

Operations

I've had quite a few of those. One operation for a squint I had, that was overcompensated. I was seeing double apparently at times. They tightened one side and made sure the vision was right. I now don't have binocular vision. I can't see anything from far distances very well. Not a problem because I've never seen any different. It was around when I was four years old so as a child, you don't know any better.

I had a couple of other operations too. My feet were off the ground all the time, I walked on my toes quite a bit. I couldn't bend my legs either so I had to have an operation on the back of my knee. The side effect of increasing my mobility through multiple operations was that it had now created a phobia of hospitals for me.

So, the lasting memories I have are not of the operations but the smell of the ether in the gas mask. I tended to think that someone was trying to murder me. When you're so young, you don't understand that that is not the case. I felt as though someone was following me with this ether mask; I seemed to think that I was being gassed. I knew it was for my own good. It's had the desired effect mobility wise along with everything else. It has got better. I used to be in a place where I got into cold sweats when even trying to ring the doctor but it got better after my hypnosis sessions. I exercise at the gym regularly, so it's not like I'm sick or ill often so I've managed to avoid the hospitals like the plague. I could go and visit whoever it was I needed to see but I couldn't go for myself.

I never wanted my diagnosis of having Cerebral Palsy to place limitations on what I could do and so it never has. I've always been a happy-go-lucky kid who had the whole world in front of me.

Never be ashamed or afraid of your mess. Without a mess, you wouldn't have a message.

In Praise of Dustbins (A Tribute to Plettaid)

Why Write a Poem about a Dustbin?
Dustbins are not grand
Yes, on the face of it
The reason is hard to understand
But Dustbins are essential
They are containers for rubbish you see
Not only empty Cans of Coke
The odd empty Carton of Milk
Or the left-over Bags
From last night's shopping Spree
Let me tell you my story
Then perhaps you will understand
Why I value Dustbins so highly
Even though they are not grand
My story starts in December
On a winter's Night
I went out to an Abba Tribute Concert
It was BRILLIANT!
Everything then felt so Right
But little did I know
While I was enjoying the Party
My Mum became very sick
Certainly, she wasn't feeling so hearty
After a couple of months
Mum passed away
I knew she was free from suffering
But that didn't take the Pain away
I was in a state –
Not knowing how to feel
What to think,

Or even if I wanted to stay
My friends tried to help – they comforted me
But a way out of my Fog of Bewilderment
I simply couldn't see
After a while
I went on holiday
To Plettenberg Bay
I'd been there often
But this year
I had a new Place to Stay
I went to Cornerway House
To stay with Robin and Dee
I felt a great sense of Peace
The Love and Acceptance healing me
I learned about Invicta House
Where hurting People went to stay
When Life had kicked them in the Teeth
As a result
They'd Lost their way
Everyone I met
Seemed so happy
What a Place to have Found
The only thing was
Children Lived there with their Mothers
They Played on the Grass
Where there was rubbish on the Ground
That Afternoon for the first time in ages
A breakthrough happened for me
Sitting outside enjoying the Sun
Quite Suddenly
God Broke through the fog
Covering my Heart and Mind

He caused me to see
That I could affect the lives of others
It wasn't all about me
I knew there had to be a change
Starting from that Moment- right there and Then
I Understood it was a defining moment
Time for my life to begin again
Suddenly I had an urge
An urge to buy a Bin
A Dustin – a place for the people living in invicta House
To put their Rubbish in
It might have been only a Bin
But it was just the start
Of a complete new outlook on life
For me a complete renewal of Heart
At the end of my holiday
I went home with a New Spirit
I would raise Funds for Plettaid
I would put my Heart and Soul in it
First, came a sponsored Silence
Which was a miracle in Itself
I'm challenged in Mobility
So, I enjoy chatting – I had to keep quiet
To make lots of wealth!
Then came a Sponsored Cycle– on this I was in a spin
I could not ride a Bike – that's where God's Grace Came in
Now – Believe it or not I walk on the Treadmill
Oh, What a BALL
When I started on this training
I could hardly walk at all!
Thank you, Lord, for everything you do
The Miracles I have Seen

Take one Dustbin
God's Love and
A vision of the Heart
Then you have all the Ingredients
Necessary to make a completely fresh Start!

Claire Bloomfield (15th August 2010)

Candles – A Sign of Hope

What do you see when you look at a Candle?
First impressions may not be much
Candles are Just sticks with Wicks
They have no Inherent Beauty
There is nothing good to touch

A Candle can lie for years
Of no apparent use in a Drawer
It's only when there is a Power Cut
We find out what our Candle is for

When it is really dark
Our Candle comes into its own
When we Light the Wick
It Shines bright
To illuminate the scene
It dispels the darkness –
To give us hope
Where once only
Despair and Gloom have been

We can all go through times
When we feel Sad, and Alone
When Nothing is Changing
We've tried everything we've ever Known
It's then we need our Candles
We all have them – it's true
Our Candles are all different
But they Bring us through

A Candle could Be encouragement
From a Friend
Or that time with Family
You promised to spend
It can be something very small and
Apparently Insignificant
To all but the one who will See

So when you feel discouraged
Do not Despair
Light the Candle
Share your Heart with God
He is Closer than your Faintest Prayer

Claire Bloomfield
(12th February 2012)

'Strangers are friends we haven't met yet.'

Claire Bloomfield

Chapter Three

IDENTITY

The Growth Matrix

As compared to the outside, identification is on the inside. Most individuals identify themselves on the outside based on their colour, their faith and their environment, all of the external factors that make them believe that they are who they are.

If you don't have inner peace; if you don't know how to build an internal core growth program, then it's really hard to self-actualise who you are because you haven't even begun. You have no base for development and growth.

I think individuals will change constantly. I think they will improve based on being mindful and having the opportunity to change. I also believe there is a phase of transition. Some may start off being right-brained at the beginning of their life journey and then transition into someone who is left-brained or vice versa. If you are more visionary, innovative and emotional, you would be classified as right-brained. Whereas if you're more logical, more detailed, more of a critical thinker, an organised person, then you're classified as left-brained. So you could be either right-brain dominant or left-brain dominant. Often, you can't do very well if you're just a visionary type of person.

If you want to achieve something, you can imagine it happening but you can't actually make it happen. And then you concentrate on organisational lines if you are a left-brained person; you can remain in the specifics but you have no *'big picture,'* so to say; you can't get out of the rut. It's paralysis by analysis sometimes, as they say. So, the genius is that you can place the left brain with the right brain so that you can have a whole-brain that helps you to understand how to do things. This is the most important part to me for when you want to work out who you want to become, who you are and how you're going to realise the ability for yourself.

Teenage Years

I liked being 15 years old as I did my Duke of Edinburgh award. I seemed to succeed in a lot of things when I was 15.

When I was 17 I went to Penarth, South Wales, to attend The Salvation Army Music School for people with disabilities, for a whole week. The week consisted of workshops for Choir and Band practice. It included a day out visiting Ross on Wye; we also had entertainment in the evening.

The week culminated in a concert for friends and family. During this time, I met Ira, who has become like a sister to me. When we met, I was very insecure and unsure of myself. Ira, in my mind, was the first person who valued me for myself. She taught me to read music, to realise my own worth but most importantly; we had FUN! We are still good friends to this day even though we don't see each other very often.

Up to that point, I felt no different from anyone else. However, all that changed when I started college at the age of 17. I had all of the ordinary difficulties of a teenager. Although I enjoyed school and felt much protected there, I don't think the environment did me any favours. Going from such a nurturing place, like the school I was previously in, to a place of such open competition, was an extraordinarily bruising experience.

In personal identity, I had huge issues because I felt nobody understood me. I was arguing a lot with people. Arguing with my

Mum a lot and every now and then she used to say to me,

"You were such a nice young child; now you've become really awful and difficult."

It's not what you need to hear as a teenager; you need to feel built up. We used to argue a great deal. We couldn't be in a room with each other without arguing for five minutes. Fortunately, now I've worked out that we must have been so similar to each other which was the real reason why we used to argue so much. It was just such a difficult time when I was in my teens.

Things were so different from school, I realised I was growing up for a start and things were happening to me that I couldn't control. It's the realisation that you're not a child anymore but again you're not an adult either. You don't feel understood. When I had my period, I was not happy at all. I remember feeling scared to use the bathroom just in case I bled.

My mum rang the school and told them what was going on. So, I had a lot of support from them, I was 11 years old at the time and remember feeling quite cheated that this had happened now to me. I wasn't happy at all. Puberty and emotions hit along with the question; 'Why me?'

I felt that I didn't have people to talk to. I couldn't test the waters with anybody and felt I didn't have someone to confide in. I just think I didn't bother. I felt I should be able to manage as Mum had taught me not to ask for anything and so I ended up managing on my own but not actually managing.

The Spastic Society

Before I left school when I was 16, I attended a five-day assessment with "The Spastic Society". On the basis of purely having Cerebral Palsy, they told me that I wouldn't cope at college.

When I felt ready and then someone says that actually I wasn't capable enough, it made me feel incapable. It knocked back my confidence to the next level.

They said I wouldn't cope in a college with only able-bodied students. It's not what I need to be told when I was only 16 years of age. They said it would be a culture shock going from an environment that protected me to a nonprotective one and that I wouldn't manage by myself. I went to a college of able people. It put negativity in my mind and I automatically felt I couldn't cope.

In college, I felt suicidal. All I was doing was crying at home. I couldn't express my feelings and others used to tell me that that is just how it is. I felt like I couldn't openly say to anyone that I couldn't handle things because I just had to take it. You could not say that you couldn't manage as you have to be able to. The crowds of people frightened me, the fear of not being able to be in with the crowd or able to fit in haunted me. Along with the safety issues too, as well as the different expectations that college has on you.

Finding your way around the place, the pressure was too much. Books I had to carry around. I used to go to French for two hours in the afternoon. You go from there to full time, you can't make proper friends. You can't hang out with someone personally. It was more the emotional shock at the time. In the school I was in before I was part of the majority, I was in the minority in college.

As soon as they find out that you have a disability, there's the barrier of overprotection and then not being understood. Some would just make assumptions.

Admittedly college was difficult, although the lecturers were very kind and did so much to help me. It was a real culture shock. Despite the difficulty, I proved them wrong.

Imagine being a bird and having a warm nest to live in and suddenly being thrown out and told you have to look after yourself. It was so frightening. In fact, at college, I experienced thoughts of death as I would go to bed at night and pray not to wake up again. I believe that I didn't act on my thoughts because I didn't want to let God or my family down.

The Spastic Society, whose attitude taught me to be someone of encouragement and support, gave only negative input, which I know coloured my thoughts for a very long time. Indeed, I still have to constantly fight feelings of insecurity and inadequacy to this day, although not nearly so much.

I believe that my experience at College started badly and continued to worsen. As a result of my involvement with The Spastic Society, I entered college with the idea that I wouldn't cope. Consequently, this belief became my really sad reality in my eyes because in the time preceding leaving school, I had felt as if my life was coming together. It was a real wake up call. I had felt much protected in school but now I was on my own. Although the lecturers were very good to me, I felt like a fish out of water, very alone and quite suicidal, not wanting to wake up again. This was compounded by the negative mindset that had been instilled into me.

I even had driving lessons which were an experience on their own; driving to me represented total freedom. The thought of never having to rely on people for lifts was a great goal, one I pursued for eighteen months. Unfortunately, due to my eyesight problem, I could not continue but I never regretted trying.

I did quite well in my exams, gaining a B for O level English and a C for O level French. As an extracurricular activity, I took up the guitar, which was very enjoyable but I can't make a career out of it! I used to skip lectures that I was either bored with or felt I couldn't cope with.

Finding My Identity

I struggled with my identity for quite a while because I was always just seen as someone's daughter or friend. I didn't have my own identity for some time. It's only in my teenage years I actually started to get my own identity and didn't feel as though I was separate from other people but they were very difficult times for me. Being 15 years of age was good but being a teen at college was very hard and that gave me more of an identity than anything. I struggled with just being separate from people because I just didn't realise that I had my own identity.

It happened to me when my Nan died; she was 95 years old when she died. My Nan and my Granddad had been part of my life forever. My Grandad died in 1996, and my Nan died when I was 40 years old.

It was about 18 years ago now so I remember sitting there with Nan and praying for her because she was going to die. She had a stroke and she was no longer the same person. So, I said to her,

"If you want to be with Grandad, go and be with Grandad; that's why I am praying".

That's when I realised that she was going to die. People have been taken off the train one by one. The more people who are taken off the train, the more you realise you have your own identity. You have to grow, not to get rid of the space but you have to grow into what you've left you.

My Nan and Grandad gave me the biggest present, which was my faith. This played a huge role for me. The more people who boosted my relationship with God, the more people that I could now rely on, the more you think you have to step up to the plate now. I used to think life was a rehearsal of things. I think I lived in a safety bubble.

When my Nan died I realised that life was not a rehearsal and this is the only time we get. I decided that I wanted to do something with my life; I wanted to go places. So, I moved out of home, I went on holiday; I just knew I had to take the bull by the horns and do what I wanted to do. This is not a practice for something that's going to go on later. This is not a rehearsal, you are actually experiencing life for real and you have to make the most of it.

Emotional Challenges – Jealousy

I was very protective of my Grandad. When Sarah (my cousin) was born, I was only 11 years old and I just remember my Mum telling me that my Uncles' wife was going to have a baby. I was like, 'I'm not impressed with that because my Grandad is my Grandad.' I didn't want to share him with anybody. I used to be quite unsure of myself to the point that if someone I loved, loved someone else then they won't love me anymore. I didn't realise at the time that love is elastic and you can take more people and things in. It doesn't mean that because one person loves another person, they can't love anyone else. It may have had something to do with the fact I was only a child. So that took me a while to wrap my head around. However, it didn't change anything in terms of my relationship with my Grandad but at the time, I thought it might have.

Faith

I was brought up to attend The Salvation Army, as was my Mum and her parents before her had. I had a very close bond with my maternal grandparents and always felt that they understood me. This was extremely important as I have spent a lot of my life trying to *fit in* and feeling very out of place. I believe that my Nan and Grandad were my emotional foundation, if you like. We always enjoyed being together and were able to share feelings at a very deep level. They would consistently visit on a Friday evening when we would pray together before I went to bed. I am convinced that this is how God became very accessible to me, someone I saw as my friend.

One of my favourite parts of the day was the evening after tea, when I could retreat to my bedroom, play my music and talk to God. This may sound strange but I always felt that He was with me, someone that no-one else could see. I knew I could talk to him about everything and that He understood. I wasn't sure at that time why or how God could love me (because I didn't like myself at all) but I just knew He did. Just recently, I received a huge revelation concerning this – let me try to explain.

Because I didn't like myself, I reasoned that I was not acceptable or good enough to have friends (although I got on very well with my friends, the relationship between my Mum and myself was shaky; we argued a lot). My perception at this point in my life was that I was difficult. I have since been shown that I am not difficult; I was carrying feelings that did not belong to me.

When I was 16 years old, after much nagging on my part, my parents bought me a puppy. She was only 8 weeks old, all head and legs. She was an American Cocker Spaniel with beautiful silver buff fur. I named her Honey. She was my best companion, always pleased to see me when I came home. She became very excited on Sunday mornings and enjoyed her outings to the stables, always staying close to my horse.

I was completely devastated when my dog Honey died aged 12. In fact, Honey's death brought my faith crashing to the ground.

I should explain that at the age of 15, I made a personal commitment to God as a result of visiting a friend at The Salvation Army Training college. Chris was a friend of mine from the salvation army who went to the training college to become a minister in the church at the army training college.

One day I went to visit her there as going to the army training college was one of my ambitions, especially to become an officer. It wasn't a practical decision for me really. When I visited my friend there, it made me take a head decision to be enrolled in the church and decide to be a part of the church. I recognised that this was the right decision. I knew I wanted to follow Jesus but the realisation that he loved me for myself, had not permeated my heart.

That happened whilst I was at college. I watched the film *'Joni'*. This is the true story of Joni Erickson – Tada. A 17-year-old from Maryland who dived into a shallow pool and broke her neck, rendering her a Quadriplegic. It was so inspirational. I then had my experience of God at that time. I had a verse of a song stuck in my head, *"Have thy own way"* and had the feeling that God was speaking to me because watching that film was so powerful. This film had a profound effect on me. I had the words of a song repeating over and over again in my head;

"Have Thine own way Lord Have Thine own way, Thou art the Potter, and I am the Clay. Mould me and make me after thy will. While I am waiting yielded and Still."

From that moment, I knew I had to give Jesus my Life. Until the death of Honey, I had what I considered to be a strong relationship with God. However, when she died, I became very angry with Him. If He knew how much I needed Honey why did he allow her to die? At the same time, one of my Dad's friends was very ill with Alzheimer's disease. Consequently, I cut myself off from The Salvation Army.

The emotional effects of cerebral palsy are often a result of feeling misunderstood or alone. Adverse emotional effects like withdrawn behaviour, anxiety, depression, or angry outbursts are commonly experienced as a result of motor impairments.

Faith is really important to me, and I don't think I would be here right now writing this book without it, even though it's been a sea-saw of a ride. Coming out of my latest Toby crisis, who was my cat who disappeared one day. One day he was there but the next day he wasn't. I was so upset about it as I always used to call him inside every evening. He'd come in around 6pm for his food and he liked his own comfort.

It was December 2018 this particular morning and when I came downstairs, he was there, so I stroked him and then gave him some food and then he went out through the cat flap and then I never saw him again. Pippa's army looked for him by putting posters up. But looking at it now, I've concluded that he was going on 14 years old, so possibly he wasn't very well that day. I used to say to God, 'Why did you let him disappear like this?' I don't know what happened to him at all. I had to live with it really. I did as much as I could for him. He shouldn't have been the most difficult cat to find as he only had three legs. He would have come back if he could have done it. I set the alarm clock by his meowing outside the door.

Sometimes, we don't always have the answers to everything, and life just has to go on. With all these ups and downs in life, there are stages where I felt that my disability had let me down. However, there were times that even though I thought God had let me down, I still felt he was right there beside me, pulling me through the rollercoaster of life.

I want to share an experience I had some years ago. It was the first time I had conscious proof of God's love and care for me. I had gone to Spring Harvest in Minehead with friends from Church. Spring harvest is a five-day conference usually held around Easter time. Anyway, this particular day I had booked to go to a talk that I was interested in with a friend. The friends I was staying with in the chalet had already gone out to the various activities. The friend I was going with was meeting me outside the chalet. I walked around the chalet, wondering how I would negotiate the chalet steps, in fact, one quite huge step. I wasn't worried but I just was mindful. Anyway, I went to the door and my friend was already outside. She could not help me as although her walking was much better than mine, she had very little balance. So, as I went to the door, the door to the opposite chalet started creaking. Then it was opened and the chap who was there came out! I felt so blessed as I had been asking how I would negotiate the steps and now here was the help I needed straight away!!! I asked whether he would mind giving me a hand and he was only too happy to!! It was a blessing in disguise as all I had to do was ask full-heartedly and it happened, as though God is listening to everything we say and watching over everything we do.

Music School

I attended a music school that was run by the salvation army. We used to have drama, music and choir practice with games and chatting. This is where I met my best friend. I love a bit of drama and would have loved to have gone to drama school. Meeting this friend of mine opened me up to a new world of possibilities. I went to college in September and met her in July and she was definitely one of the most positive things that happened to me. She taught me to read music and she just understood me. It was the type of friendship where you can always connect at any time. You can pick up where you left off.

These types of friendships are very rare to find. I found it difficult to connect with people, or more like I shut myself out, blindly thinking that people wouldn't understand me or just felt as though I had to manage with so many mixed emotions. It's only when my loved ones had passed away that I felt that I actually did have my own identity, I was Claire Bloomfield and I was unique in many ways, with great abilities of my own.

Fear is (A Poem)

False evidence appearing real
There is no doubt about how it can make you feel
Sweaty palms, a dry mouth, voices in your head saying no
It's true the only thing that seems right – is to just leave
everything and go

But… Everything that fear says is a lie-The thing is do you want
to get past it? Do you want to fly?
When the urge to fly overtakes your fear, you will succeed.
When you give in to fear in yourself, it will just breed
I'm not saying it's Easy, but when fear is at its height
Calm your mind, control your thoughts; it will take flight.

When you are in a place where it seems there is nothing left to do –
take control of your fear
Don't let it take control of you.

Claire Bloomfield (28th August 2014)

Choices - A Mind's Eye View

I am faced with choices every single day
What to think
How to Feel
What to Say
There are so many voices telling me what to do
I really don't know how to silence them
What should I do?
That was me - until Today - I had a revelation - Hey
Only I have the Key to unlock my Potential
This is my Revelation
don't you see?
I am in charge of my Destiny
Me and only Me.
When the voice of Fear comes knocking -
I can Listen - If I choose, but it is a Lie.
Fear feeds on the power I allow it to have - I have the power to kill
it, it must die
I saw change as a negative thing but change is here to stay - change
leads to progress - there is no other way
This is only part of what I learnt from the Treadmill Today - for a
piece of plastic, it has a lot to say!
I know there is more on another day - wait this is not the biggest
thing in any way -
It told me when I feel Small daunted and in fear - I should ignore
those feelings - They cost me far too dear
I am unique - A one-off - I was born to Shine
To greet Success with a smile
Because it is mine!

Claire Bloomfield (1st September 2014)

'Our deepest fear is not that we are inadequate; it's that we are powerful beyond measure.
It's our light, not our Darkness that most frightens us...'

Marianne Williamson

Chapter Four

STRUGGLE

The Butterfly Effect

The concept of the butterfly is spectacular, especially in how it emerges from the cocoon. It's a horrendous and painful process.

Even though I've seen myself as someone who looks on the positive side of things, life has been a struggle to come to terms with. I mentioned it in my previous chapter in regards to having fits. Even though they didn't define me, they were a part of my life when I was younger, which made me feel different from the other children. Everyone had some form of disability at school, so you don't tend to think and feel you fit in. But it was the episodes of fits when I was younger that made me feel quite alienated from the other children as I didn't understand why I was getting them. I never felt different from my friends as I never thought of it like that, I suppose.

I remember being quite surprised when a neighbour of mine in her 70s went into the hospital, which was the first time she had been in. It just astounded me as to how someone could come so far in life and not have visited a hospital in her lifetime as it was the norm for me.

My college days were the most challenging for me as it was such a culture shock in so many ways. In many ways, we are all like butterflies. The transformation process from a caterpillar into a butterfly is so magnificent. Still, we tend to not see the struggles in between as the outcome is so beautiful in so many ways.

As the lowly caterpillar or larva goes through a metamorphosis process to become what is going to be a lovely butterfly one day, something extraordinary happens.

The larval phase, also known as the resting phase, switches to the pupa phase. A great deal of change is happening underneath the surface, despite what its name might imply.

Most of the tissues and cells that make up the larva inside the pupa are broken down during this time and that material is rebuilt into the adult form; the butterfly. The wings are pressing and pushing, pushing against the inside of the pupa as the butterfly reaches its moment of release and liberty, when it will eventually be able to fly. It is the pushing motion that strengthens the butterfly's wings so that it can fly when it is ready to emerge. It wouldn't be powerful enough to fly if we were to take a pair of scissors or a knife and split open the cocoon prematurely before the butterfly was ready.

Its struggle strengthens the butterfly. There're not many times in our lives when we feel like crying, *"Now is the time!"* Or *"I'm wary of waiting!"* We wonder when we will be able to see our efforts paying off. This attitude of *"I want it now"* and *"I don't want to miss it"* permeates our culture and is something I constantly struggle with.

I'm reminded of the butterfly's journey and its process of transformation and strength building in those moments. It can only take flight only when the butterfly is ready and has built up its power.

Caterpillars have no idea that they are going to become butterflies. Now think about that for a bit. The caterpillar doesn't know that it's going to be turned into a magnificent, colourful, fascinating being; just like we don't know what's in store for our lives.

Often, we can feel tiny and insignificant but what if we're getting ready for something bigger, something that we can't even understand? We never know what our humble beginnings could inspire us to do one day.

To empower you, prepare you for what you are supposed to do and who you are meant to be, think about what is being brought into your life. In your struggle, can you find strength? We may be on the threshold of our biggest moment, on the brink of *"arriving,"* and not even know it. We could have been so close.

So, trust the process. Stick to hope and you will be given the power you need to spread your wings and fly when you are ready, when your time comes.

Each part of life teaches us life lessons to help overcome those challenges to help us evolve into a beautiful butterfly. I hold no regrets with any of my life experiences as each and every one has taught me a lesson and helped me to better myself and become the person I am today; resilient, independent and a driven woman who's able to have the mindset to overcome any challenges or struggles that are thrown my way.

There was a time when I was in nursery and the snow was falling heavily and I looked out of the window thinking, *"I have to get to school"*. There's a bus that picked us up and took us to school but it wasn't coming on this particular day, so we didn't have any transport to get into school. So, I forced my Dad to drive me there because I didn't want to miss out. I found to my astonishment, that I was the only one who had made the effort to come in on a snow day. I was completely spoiled that day. It felt so surreal to believe that I had that ambitious mindset at a young age to be unstoppable; nothing would come in my way of getting to where I wanted to be. I just had to put my mind to it to achieve it. As many people couldn't find a way to get in, I was so determined to go in and not miss out that I made it happen.

I remember once I was with this teacher and she had told me that I was going up a year to be with another teacher, Mrs Brown's class. Every day since she told me that I used to nag her, asking whether it was time yet for me to go to Mrs Brown's class because I was so excited about going to this other teachers' class. The teacher I was with first was very strict and I found Mrs Brown to have a softer personality. I just wanted to get away, to be in a place that I felt comfortable and free.

I used to love the rope ladder in school even though it was dangerous, the thrill of it just excited me. I loved taking calculated risks. It takes bravery to face the fear of uncertainty, to take a chance to reach a goal. Either way, we evolve through the process and become more resilient and optimistic, no matter the outcome. Better still, developing these abilities allows us to take more risks and increases the chances of achieving future objectives. This has definitely been one of my driving forces in life.

I had a really good friend called Anne; her disability was that she only had one lung and she used to say that she wanted about six children so I used to tell her,

"Oh no, I wouldn't want to have six children or even want to have one".

She fancied this boy, she ran after him and I always used to have to say, *"Leave him alone!"* as I knew he wasn't interested and I didn't want her to get her heart broken. I couldn't bear not speaking to her. If we ever fell out, I always used to approach her and say,

"Can we start talking again?" as I couldn't bear the thought of losing her as a friend. I couldn't bear having any bad blood between us so I used to go up to her and say,

"Can't we just make up now, can't we just be friends again? Because I don't like it without you."

It can be a daunting moment for anyone to transition into adulthood but young adults with CP face extra particular challenges. One of the biggest problems I faced in college was the perception of my disability among people. It was easy for me as a teen with CP to get ignored, discouraged or even patronised simply because I was not considered *'normal'*.

The Angel & The Demon

During my teenage years, I used to have to separate myself from myself. I used to feel like the disability was nothing to do with me and thought I could park it in one place and carry on. But actually, I couldn't. I used to blame everything I felt on an imaginary friend who followed me everywhere, chipping away at me with her problems. Anything that happened was all her. So, if I was angry, it was her. If I was upset, it was her.

She was just a screaming child who just kept on screaming constantly. I just couldn't get rid of her. She was literally just a screaming child who just made me so mad. I used to relate my disability to her. I wasn't able to put a face or image to her until my hypnosis sessions. I always knew there was someone there as I've always looked at my disability as a screaming child that I took everywhere with me. All I wanted to do was leave it behind. It just used to sit on the floor and scream all the time. It's like what you'd do with a naughty child. You'd say,

"If you misbehave anymore, then I'll just leave you there screaming!"

At the time, she was a faceless and nameless child who just sat there and screamed the whole time. She just wanted to do her own thing and go her own way.

During my teenage years, I felt no one really understood me and couldn't speak to anybody about anything. I always felt like I had to cope with everything all the time. I've always thought you had to manage and you can't ask for help. At the time, I felt as though I was devalued and that I couldn't succeed in anything. The only really good time was how much I loved being 15 years old, as the Duke of Edinburgh award was my great accomplishment.

I never took the blame for anything. It was always the naughty child that was playing up again. My disability was just a naughty child that I wanted to send away but it wouldn't go away because it's there permanently. Most of the time, I could calm it down but the child would mainly come out when I was frustrated.

I remember going to Holland with a friend of mine to stay with another friend of mine. While we were there, we went to a Dutch lady's house. The house was called Corrie Ten Boom and was used to shelter many Jews during the war and so their home had been made into a museum you could go and visit. I had been looking forward to this trip and viewing everything they'd set up in the museum, it was one of the things I really wanted to do.

We got there and it wasn't big enough for me to get into with the wheelchair. Well, I just threw my toys out of the pram, so to say. I had made it all this way and I couldn't get in. I was fuming with rage and disappointment and there it was; the child again screaming away. I felt so discriminated against. I was so angry and frustrated as it was just another thing that I couldn't do. I was a spoilt young adult then. Why should everyone else be able to do that and not me? I wanted to experience it for myself. It was times like these that my disability stopped me from doing legitimate things. It was a small place and they didn't make any adjustments to it as it was still the way it was in the times when they sheltered the Jews. So, if they changed it, it wouldn't be authentic. I understood that was why I couldn't view it but not doing something that I had really put my heart and soul into seeing, well I couldn't have that. Nowadays, you can get an online tour but back then, it wasn't available. I just thought it was something I really wanted to do but then I had to miss out on it. We got there on time and still they said,

"Sorry, we don't have the facilities for you to go in."

I was so cross for the rest of that afternoon as I felt that that was the end for me. During times like this, the demon who was that inner child would be knocking away, saying,

"Look, that's another thing you can't do all because of this disability."

Every time I felt angry, upset, frustrated or sad, this child would just appear and I would blame all my emotions on this screaming child.

As I mentioned before, it was only during my hypnosis sessions that I could put a face and name to this child. She was my coping mechanism. The disability had nothing to do with me. I used to blame everything I felt on her. During a session, I saw this blonde-haired, blue-eyed child who was only 8 years old and when the hypnosis lady asked me what my imaginary friend was called, I said *"Amelia."* And she said,

"That's right; it's in the middle, so really it's an inner child version of you."

That's only when I found out that Amelia and myself were one person. Amelia was my inner child who I was blaming and she represented everything bad about my disability. The things I couldn't do or express.

But now I can mould her and me together and take responsibility for the fact and say,

"Yes, I'm upset but I can own it", or

"Yes, I feel sad but I can own it."

I didn't need to push those feelings away because they were there for a reason. That's the reason why she has disappeared, more or less. Every now and again, she'll be around but definitely not as much.

On the other hand, I had my so-called angel, who was named Susan. Susan was around in my early thirties. I saw her in my bedroom at my flat. She wasn't always around - she always came on shopping trips, especially if I was with my Mum and Dad. Susan was a tool to diffuse arguments, especially between my Mum and me. I didn't have her at home only when we went out.

She would always support me - my Mum and Dad didn't know about her because she was never home, only when we were out. I met Amelia sometime after Susan left. Once I didn't need her emotionally, she left. I saw Amelia under hypnosis. I had always known she was there, just not seen her. Susan was an imaginary friend, similar to Amelia. However, she only appeared when I was out and about and never when I was inside. Amelia tried to be a friend but because she represented everything wrong with my disability, I literally pushed her away in the early years.

Susan was the angel and Amelia was the devil. They were both my ways of expressing myself. Amelia was my inner child. However, I didn't actually meet her until I was 33 years old. I always knew that she existed. I just didn't see her face or know her name. She stood for everything I hated, my lack of mobility and frustration. She was a coping mechanism; I met her, as you know, at 33 through hypnosis - I believe at a time when I was ready to acknowledge and face myself and gradually heal by fusing the two of them together with me.

Susan was there to stop arguments with my Mum when we were out and about. As I've mentioned before, my relationship with my Mum was quite shaky. We used to argue a lot and never see eye to eye. This merely could have been due to the fact we both had similar personalities that would cause us to often clash on viewpoints. My Mum, during my teenage years, found me quite difficult to control. She even said,

"When did you become like this? You were so well behaved before," and this got to me because I knew I hadn't changed. I just felt as though no one understood where I was coming from and no one could see my viewpoint. I found it very difficult to express myself. This is when Susan would appear and she would be my angel to give me a shoulder to lean on, to support me when I needed. I didn't feel so alone when she was around. I didn't tell anyone about her but I felt that she had my back. She was around when we were out and about. I used to call her to come out with us. She disappeared when we were indoors. Susan has gone now, I don't see her any more. Amelia has now grown into an adult and she is much more helpful.

Amelia

Amelia is a lovely girl
She is aged eight
If you continue
To read this Poem
You'll understand why
I think she's great

Amelia is a lively child
Oh she loves to play
She just loves to run
Jump, Dance and skip
All day

I first met Amelia
When I was Thirty-Three
I had no idea
Why she came
Or what her role would be

At first, I didn't like Amelia
To be honest
I didn't even
Know her name
All she did was
Lie on the floor and Scream
I hated her behaviour
Now I realise
I was to blame

You see Amelia and I
Are the same person
She and I are one
My mind created her
Because I resented my disability
I thought nothing could be done

In the past two weeks
I've met Amelia
Given her a name
Seen her face
In my mind's eye I've seen her
She is a well-behaved child
Blonde-haired blue-eyed
Amelia is a child
I finally can embrace

I saw Amelia
As out of control
I know now
This wasn't the case
Because I couldn't love myself
For Amelia there was no place

Amelia craved attention and acceptance
Which I felt unable to give
Now I love Amelia
She is me after All
I know beyond doubt
I'm Acceptable and Accepted
Whole with or without Her

I'm set free
To walk proud and Tall

Claire Bloomfield (27th February 2017)

Amelia Again

Amelia's been around Today
She is still only eight
But now when we meet
She's more compliant
Does what she's told
Which for me is just great

I've told her
There's no advantage
In lying on the floor to scream
All that happens
When she does is
She gets ignored
Or people walk away
So now she behaves like a dream

Amelia may only be eight
But she's learnt how to
Reason, to explain her emotions
When she's angry or in pain
I'm so glad she knows for certain
That in bad behaviour
There is nothing to gain

There are so many similarities

Between Amelia and myself
I'm so glad she is part of my life
Because with her lies wisdom -
Such a wealth

You will be aware
If you read the previous poem
That Amelia and I are
One and the same
To think I spent a long time
Pushing her away
It seems such a shame
However, I have talked to Amelia
She understands
That when I was young
I had trouble expressing my emotions too
I blamed her for my life
She spoilt my plans

Last night I had a revelation
Far from being a hindrance
Because she has matured
Amelia could help me deal
With emotions I didn't like
Or want
but were none the less Real

I'm grateful to Amelia
For being part of me
For giving me clarity
Setting me free

Helping when things are
Beyond my control
I love you Amelia
Spirit, Body and Soul

Claire Bloomfield (17th March 2017)

Amelia continued...

Today I saw Amelia
As an adult
She had Poise Confidence and Grace
Gone was the Screaming Child
With the bad Behaviour and
The Angry face

Today when I saw Amelia
I realised we could be
Together as one
I didn't need to separate her from me

I admit I didn't want Amelia
To Grow up
I've always seen her
As Eight
But that is not reality
Fantasy is fun
For a while
But permanently
It's never a solution
Just gets you in a state

I only caught a glimpse
Of Amelia
As an adult
Before that she was still
A Child
Playing in the Garden
Running about and
Going Wild
It may have
Only been a glimpse
But a glimpse
Was enough to see
What it would be like
To let Amelia
Grow up to be
The person she was
Always meant to be

When I thought about it Before
I thought growing up would
Mean I would lose her
But growing up means
Amelia is set free
We will always be together
Because we're part
Of Each other
Amelia and I

The truth is that because we are one
Living with Amelia
Will always be fun

Amelia can be anything
I want her to be
Sometimes an Adult
At other times a child
Enjoying life
Running free and wild

If I draw any lesson from Today
It would be
That I never have
To push Amelia away
Or be ashamed of the Child within me
I now understand and I can see
I am whole -
I can succeed at being me

Claire Bloomfield (26th April 2017)

'Real isn't how you're made. It's a thing that happens to you. Sometimes it hurts, but when you're real, you don't mind being hurt. It doesn't happen all at once. You become once you are real you can't be ugly except to people who don't understand. Once you are real, you can't become unreal again. It lasts for always.'

Margery Williams
The Velveteen Rabbit

Chapter Five

BULLYING

The Boxing Match

As mild as my case of CP may be, there were always the high bullies who found pleasure in bringing me down. Sometimes it felt that the only reason they were there that day was to be my rain cloud, following me around pointing out my mistakes and flaws. A bully does not compare to what you're emotionally putting yourself through—only entertaining the idea that you're not the same as anyone else will work against anyone, even though you know in so many respects that you're above the average.

However, when people got to me, there were moments when their harassing and hurtful comments started to penetrate. I even found myself thinking a few times, 'What if they were right?' I have since found this to be the toughest emotional place I had to dig myself out of. But I told myself what I knew was true:

"You're the right one!"

Whatever they think, you know you're better than them. Only because you're not going to resort to behaving like them, they make you feel like an outcast, so that after all, their pitiful lives may not seem so meaningless.

"Someone Like You."

I got to know a disability employment officer who pointed me to the community programme. That was a programme for people who had been unemployed for a long time. It was one of my first jobs and our project was to insulate elderly people's houses in the winter. I did a lot of the secretarial work for that and answered the switchboard which I quite enjoyed. It was only two and a half days of work a week. About £50.00 for that job was not bad at all. I stayed in that job for about a year then got put into another job by the employment services, where the bullying started. It was the supervisor there who bullied me. She used to say things like,

"The manager shouldn't have taken on someone like you; we're carrying you."

So I said, *"Oh, really?"* and she said,

"Oh yeah, she really shouldn't have taken on someone like you, you can't manage and you have so many things to learn".

I fired back at her, saying,

"Hold on a minute, I think you're the one who has things to learn love, how do you know that you won't get knocked down by a bus one day? You are no different than me."

I was fuming; I was so angry that I reported her to the manager on a couple of occasions. The interesting thing is I know now she has had two mental breakdowns. Now I'm not saying it was coming for her from karma but I felt it was her own insecurities. She could be nice but most days, she just wasn't. When things go from bad to worse, then the days would be very long. She could be reasonable but when she decided to be unreasonable, she was very unreasonable.

My dog had died the day before that and I was like, 'Don't cry in front of her, don't get upset' but by the time I got home, I was a wreck. This was all in 1990. She never did it again to me; she thought she could get away with it and wipe the floor with me. It was awful and I remember shaking like a leaf, mainly because of the anger. I felt there was nothing I could do as she would just bully me anyway.

Suicidal Thoughts

I prayed every night, not wanting to wake up the next day. I just didn't want to go to the place that I was going to but I had to go there as I had no choice. I just didn't want to do that. I just felt alienated. I lived in a bubble before that and I wanted that back. I was rebelling against growing up. Almost as if someone had told me that I couldn't manage; so I didn't manage.

I didn't want to let my family or grandparents or God down, so I thought I just had to get on with it. One day I realised I was away from these thoughts; I had come out of it and adapted to life. I didn't confide in anyone. If I had confided in someone, I would have let myself down. At that time, I felt I had no way to get out, like being trapped in a spiders' web getting tighter and tighter.

There was a point where I had an epiphany and now I want to give back to the world and so I had come out of a really big struggle, I'd survived it.

Healing

Emotional healing in college and bullying at work makes you realise people do get it and that other people are going through this. So, by helping others, you are helping yourself. We spend so much time looking at closed doors we don't see the open ones on the other side. The healing came when I was in South Africa (which I'll get into later on in my story) sitting outside and looking into the sky after Mum died. The way out of grief is to not focus on it but to look for something better to focus on—steps to climb on to get out of the rut you are in. It's like a donkey when stuck in a well and more sand gets put on top of it; the donkey uses the negativity thrown at it to climb out. Even though there is negativity, the light is helping someone else.

The Poet Within Me

My love for writing poems was birthed from a Helen Shapiro concert; that's when the flow of writing began. She's retired now but she did gospel concerts. On this particular evening, I felt so emotional. I felt that something was there. They said you're going to be birthing something and something will happen and then the next minute I'm awake and it's two o'clock in the morning with the poem about the river in my mind. I've never written a poem before but suddenly I had to take a pen and paper to bed because I never knew when ideas would flow. This was also the start of my journey to emotional freedom as I was able to express myself through the poems and say things that I couldn't say in ordinary life. I was able to say worthwhile things. It connected me to my inner self, allowing me to express my feelings through verses. An experience that has kept me going.

.

The Journey

Today has been a Red-Letter Day
I really don't know what to say
Words are powerful
But they can't adequately express
The way I'm feeling
It's simply the Best
In these lines
I will endeavour to explain
The reason for my Joy
That I can hardly contain
Has there ever been a time
In your Life when you thought
That goal can't be reached
It's too hard
I'm Scared
My efforts will come to nought?
Well, The Treadmill was a bit like that for me
I wanted to conquer it
But a way I couldn't see
In the Beginning
I had a least three
People with me for confidence
I couldn't stand there on my own
If one of them went
I was completely thrown
Into a panic
My Legs would Fix
My mind would fly in all directions
Will I fall off or will I stay on
Take your pick

It's a journey that you have travelled with me on
Today is a different story
Best of all the sheer panic
Is all but Gone
James, The Instructor Stands at the side
Of the Treadmill to stop it to help and to guide
My biggest obstacle was incline and Speed
Separately they are accomplishable
Together? Surely I will have to concede Defeat
Today came the Breakthrough
I needed so bad
Possibly the best time on the Treadmill
I've ever had
An incline of 4.0
At a speed of 1.1
Previously something I could never have done
Not just for a minute
But a whole 5
In the past I would have been barely alive
So now you will understand
Why I'm excited
Why I feel so Grand
The Moral of my story is
If you have a dream
If you truly believe
Never give up
Let it take root and conceive
Uproot all fear and negative talk
Otherwise in it's cycle
You will be caught
With Determination, Time, Patience, Effort, Love and Grace
Not only will you dream of victory

You will look it full in the Face!

Claire Bloomfield (24th November 2014)

The Journey Part 2

I went on a long journey
I carried my suitcase for miles
It wasn't full of my clothes
But full of life's problems and trials
The road I travelled was dusty
Full of sand and stone
But I was accustomed to carrying
My suitcase completely alone
Quite suddenly I met a stranger
With me right there on the road
He was dressed in white linen
His face was a sight to behold
The stranger told me his name was Jesus
He wanted to be friends with me
He said He had died for my sake
When he was Crucified on Calvary
Something about Jesus looked familiar
He smiled as he mentioned my name
He Said
"If you give me your suitcase
Your Life will never be the Same
In that split second I realised
That this Stranger
Was sent from above
To carry the weight of my burden
To fill me with His light and love

I then handed over my suitcase
It was such a weight you see
Jesus and I linked arms
He skipped down the Road
Next to me

Claire Bloomfield

**(I wrote this a few years ago and was reminded of it this
Morning - Thank you Danni -)**

"If you give me your Suitcase
Your life will never be the same"

*'If you can't conceive it,
you won't receive it.'*

Chapter Six

CONTRIBUTION

Coming back to life

While we cannot live in a bubble to protect ourselves against the world's atrocities, we can protect ourselves and our energy. It's essential that we care for our minds and bodies on the physical plane during triggering and often confusing times. There is no one size- fits all answer for those who want more solid answers on how we can *"fix"* our problems. I'm just like you, doing the best we can do.

When I left college, I couldn't get a job for three years and lived on benefits. During this time, I did voluntary work for The Samaritans. (I realised I had gone through such a lot at college and indeed, I knew that only a miracle and God's grace had got me through it) and I wanted to do something that would be a blessing. Consequently, I applied to them with a certain amount of trepidation, not believing it would work. Imagine my surprise and delight when after eight weeks of in-house training, I was accepted. Thus began eight very happy years. I met some very special people and made some good friends. More importantly, I learnt an awful lot about life, for which I am grateful.

In between the community programme and the employment service, I worked for Christian nationals. It was a Christian sponsorship program providing sponsorship for young adults and people aspiring to the ministry in third World countries. I started with General Clerical duties and was then promoted in time to the 'sponsor a child secretary'. This entailed answering letters from sponsors about the children sending out letters to sponsors from the children and liaising with their head offices. One of my best experiences whilst working with them was going to mission 87 in Utrecht, Holland. It was a Christian conference in which we were able to have a stall detailing our work along with loads of other organisations. At first, I thought we would never get there because it necessitated a long journey that started at about five in the morning. We eventually arrived at the destination at about five in the evening!! I remember feeling very tired. Not only that but we were to sleep on mats on the floor. I also remember being very unimpressed about that too, anyway, we got there.

There was a meeting scheduled for the evening. I remember being at the meeting and feeling incredibly lonely despite the fact that there were literally thousands of people there. That was my first experience of being lonely in a crowd. I remember thinking, 'Thank goodness we are only here for a few days.' I remember that it was a really rough day because of us having to sleep on mats on the floor and there was no hot water, so there was no chance of even getting a cup of tea!

I remember living on hot chocolate from the machine until one night when a friend said there was a café across the road, so we went there. We also had a very unique alarm call in the mornings. At 6 o'clock every morning, a Dutch woman rode through the lines of mats on a bicycle. At first, it was funny but by the last day, everyone was throwing pillows at her! The funniest thing was that there was no hot water but there was a bathroom that was adapted for people with disabilities. Obviously, I used it. There was always a queue outside because people thought I had hot water!!

The alternative washing facilities were sinks on the wall. We did have some good times there. The best thing was an Adrian Snell concert, on the last evening! It was fab!! It was a music and prayer concert and lasted until 2.am!! The next day we were all tired on the trip home but it was a great night!!! The whole trip was an experience. It taught me gratitude. I would run my hand under the hot tap at home for a long time afterwards.

I also applied for various jobs, including one as a BT operator. Eventually, I got a job with the Community Programme as a switchboard operator. This position lasted a year, during which time I met the Disability Employment Advisor, who secured me a job with Christian Nationals in 1985. I stayed at this job for eighteen months, after which The Disability employment advisor secured me a position with Hornchurch Employment Service. I started this job in 1987. I did clerical work, including taking vacancies, updating the boards, imputing submissions for jobs on a computer, sending out UB85's and dealing with switchboard inquiries.

Apart from one individual who got her kicks from bullying me, as I'd already explained before in my story, I enjoyed this job. I now realise that she was insecure and this was the only way she could overcome it. I was in this employment until 1996 when I was made redundant with one other person who also had a disability. We took Hornchurch Employment Service to a tribunal in which they decided to settle out of court. I was then unemployed again.

While in this employment, I went on an R.S.A Counselling course where I met a lady called Rachel. I was drawn to her for some reason and one coffee break I shared my struggles with her. After a couple of weeks of sharing, Rachel invited me along to church with her and her husband, Les. Rachel told me that she had spoken to the Pastor, who said that it would be a very different experience for me but that I was very welcome. I accepted with pleasure. It turned out not only to be different but indeed life-changing. I went with Rachel and Les to church for two weeks. The second week was the most memorable. Everyone was walking around with flags and banners praising God and amid all the noise and activity, I heard a voice – It said,

"I want you to stay with these people."

It came a second time; this time, I was sure so I started to have a conversation with God in my head. At the end of the service, the Pastor's wife came over and asked me if I was okay. In normal circumstances, I would never talk to a stranger about my feelings, I would have just said,

"I'm fine!"

However, on this occasion, I found myself telling the truth. I told Judith how much I had enjoyed the service and I wanted whatever it was that the people had. They were so alive and God was very real. Judith then asked me if I would like to speak to her husband, Graham, the Pastor. I accepted the invitation and met with him two days later. As a result of that meeting, I joined the Church and then began one of the fastest rides of my life, spiritually speaking. The experience wasn't frightening but I felt as if I was on an out of control express train.

I thought I knew God but He began to reveal Himself in a totally new way. I started to get pictures in my mind, the first of which was a Hot Air Balloon. The Balloon was in a desert, and it rose. I felt as if God was letting me know that He understood how low I had been feeling and that He would bring healing to the hurt.

In the second picture, I saw myself standing in a field with a stream running through it. However, between the field and the stream was a wall. Being an impatient person, I wanted to do everything conceivable to remove the wall. I tried every possible way but God showed me that I couldn't move the wall but that He would dismantle it brick by brick when the time was right. It is only now that I see He has in fact gradually removed the wall throughout my life.

I was baptised into the "Havering Christian Fellowship Church" on the 12th of January 1992.

The Rainbow

I saw a beautiful rainbow
In the Sky tonight
Ok, it wasn't vibrant
But it's colours
Were there alright
The Red, Orange and Yellow
Green, Blue and Indigo
All came together
To make quite a show
I mustn't forget Violet
Of course it was there too
A Rainbow is incomplete
Without Violet's dark hue

The Rainbow taught me a powerful lesson
When I saw it in the sky
I thought about humanity -
The People we meet
Or those who pass us by

We have no idea of their circumstances
Or the Struggles they may face
That's why we have to see them
Through the eyes of Grace

It's not always easy
We can be build a wall in haste
Be quick to judge
In our mind

Think -
"I don't like them"
But on what is our decision based?
Have we taken the time to see
Who they really are
The things they have been Through
The wounds that leave their scars

The Rainbow is a powerful reminder
That diversity is vital
Because without all its colours
We could not be treated to an Eye full
Of the Rainbow's beauty and brilliance
We would never see
How spectacular its light in the sky can be

People are like Rainbows
They have different colours too
Depending on their experiences
The things that they've through
When we meet people and
Look them in the Face
May we see them truly
Through the Eyes of Love and Grace

Claire Bloomfield (31st May 2017)

Coloured Glass

I lost my coloured Glass Today
I'd had it for a while
When I looked at the colours
They used to make me smile
I used to really love this Glass
It held me in thrall
But what I didn't realise was
It was not serving me at all

You see my coloured Glass was special
It used to shine so bright
It was oh so pretty
Because it could reflect the light

I used to hold it so tightly
Because it was so precious to me
It meant so very much
Without it
Where on earth would I be

I needed to protect my coloured Glass
What was I to do
If it was to break
Then I would be in a stew

I feel now
That I need to make things clear
My "Coloured Glass"
Is a euphemism

For the Friends
That I hold dear
Certain people in my life
I know I drove them mad
All because I was insecure
Which made me feel unlovable
And so indescribably sad

A few weeks ago
I had a revelation
And I'm so happy to say
That it has meant
That I can Lose my coloured Glass
On Purpose -
Throw it completely away

I realised that friends are there
Because they want to be
I don't have to do anything
To make them stay with me

So I apologise to the friends
For whom coloured Glass
Was a strain
Thank you for still being
Part of my life
And seeing the Rainbow
Through the Rain

Claire Bloomfield (31st July 2019)

'The most important words you say in life are the words you say to yourself'

Marissa Peer

Chapter Seven

INDEPENDENCE

Gaining Emotional & Physical Freedom

My grandad's death was a huge wake-up call for me. He was 96, and he was there all my life. I didn't realise he would go; if it meant he could die, so will everyone else.

I was hit with some pretty major revelations. I was very close to my grandparents; he was my rock. It may seem unreasonable to say this now but I was not ready for him to die and I was hit by the realisation that if he could die, then other people within my support network would also not be around forever. I had to have a contingency plan, hence the flat, I realised that I needed to confront some more truths to be able to move forward.

So, I had to get myself into a situation where I could cope by myself. So, I had to be independent in my own place with them nearby if I needed them. Grandad died in January of 1996 and I moved into my flat in July. My Dad used to pick me up from work. I never told anybody I wanted to move out. I had a friend who I opened up to and I remember taking him out for the evening (he was partly my financial advisor but also a good friend who I trusted as well) and I said,

"Look, David, I don't know what to do because Grandad has died, which came as a shock for me and all. I want to be loyal to my Mum and Dad but I know I have to get a place for myself. Do you think I'm being

unreasonable?" and he said,

"No, you're not being unfair; just imagine if I took you back tonight and they weren't there, you have to make a plan."

So, I spoke to my parents about it, first of all, I put myself on the council list for a home. When my Dad came to pick me up from work one day, this particular evening, we went past this street with a new build and it said there were new flats there. And I thought, 'Really, I wonder if they have any ground floor ones?' Oblivious to me, my dad had rung them and booked a viewing time for the next day. So, we went there the next day and he did have a ground floor one. He had two actually and he showed us one at the back and one at the front near the car park. As I walked into the place I thought it felt very comfortable to me and I could really be at home here. I wanted that place and by Monday, everything was drawn up. It was an amazing feeling that I was going to get my own front door. We had one of the slowest solicitors that I had known in my life. It took from January to July, which I suppose wasn't that long but because I was so eager for something. I was over the moon when I knew I would be moving out soon. I took time off work and spent every afternoon in the flat till about 10 in the evening because I wanted to get used to it getting dark on my own. I wanted to be by myself and spend quite a lot of time over there. By that time, I used to use a wheelchair a lot when I was going out and about but I was okay not to use it indoors. I wasn't confident walking around outside, so I used to walk around indoors. Outside there were uneven pavements. It was just easier for me and everyone else.

I now realise that moving into the flat was the best thing I could have done. I'm not saying it was all plain sailing but a very necessary but steep learning curve because I had never really experienced living independently. Rather than go straight from living with my parents to living on my own, I spent five or six afternoons of the week in the flat to get used to it. Consequently, when I eventually moved in, it was far from feeling alien and different; it felt as if I was on holiday. I believe I felt secure because firstly, moving into the flat was my idea and secondly, I knew that help was near at hand should I need it. It was a proud moment when I woke up in my own home for the first time.

My Safe Haven

My excitement was so surreal; being independent and having a place to myself was a dream come true. Even before I had moved, I ensured that I had everything sorted. I had a cleaner who came to clean the house. The microwave was my saviour with the quick meals. I'm sure people thought that I would be back with my tail behind my legs, so to say, but I was definitely not going to give up, that's for sure. There was no way it wasn't going to work. It was like my child and I was pleased with my achievement. As soon as I walked through the door, I had that feeling of relief. I had no one to answer to and was able to do what I wanted to do. Nobody was saying you have to eat now or you have to go to sleep now. It was an amazing feeling.

Losing The Four Wheels

When I first did the silence sponsorship with the hand bike ride, one of my friends was going in for an induction gym session. So, she asked me,

"Do you want a lift, or are you taking the wheelchair?"

I thought, 'Do I just tell her I want the lift or do I just say I'll grab a taxi and take the wheelchair.' So, in the spur of the moment, I decided that I would leave the wheelchair behind and wanted that lift. So, I took just the sticks that day and I needed something like that to break the dependence on my chair. I needed this to break my dependency on being in the wheelchair all the time.

I used to bargain with myself as my body just wanted to sit down, so I told myself that I have to get to a certain place before sitting down. So, I used to bargain with myself every step of the way. I had to tell my mind that I only had this much to go and to keep going. It was that spur of the moment decision that gave me the freedom from the dreaded four wheels. I mainly used the wheelchair when I was out and about, purely due to the dangers around me from being pushed over by the crowds on the streets. The chair was more for convenience, and the more I relied on it, the more I became dependent on it. After the freedom from the wheelchair, I was able to rely on my sticks to get me around.

Until this stage, to manage my disability, I realised that I had separated myself from my physical body. I had rightly thought that my disability had nothing to do with me, it didn't have any bearing on who I was as a person and it still doesn't. However, to live, I needed to connect with my emotions. I saw myself as if in the supermarket with a screaming child whom I couldn't control but equally couldn't leave there. That was the beginning of my acceptance of my physical limitations.

That was and still is an ongoing process that doesn't stop, although most of the time, it is under control. In 2000 I realised I had a gift for writing poems. Most of my poems feature birds or rivers, which, to me, indicate freedom. They are also a tremendous help in releasing frustrations. I am a firm believer in not bottling things up as that just compounds issues and causes sickness. In addition to hopefully being a blessing to others, the poems have saved my life emotionally.

The Picnic Basket Poem

I saw a picnic basket
In my mind's eye
The other day
At first I was confused
I didn't know
What it meant to convey

I saw it very clearly
However, I was
In a quandary
To Explain
So here I shall Endeavour
Do my best to make it plain

My picnic basket was full
Of all sorts of different foods
Some to give you highs
And some to give you the blues

There was Tomato
There was Pasta
There was Bread
Of every Kind
You Name it
I had it
In the Basket
It was there
For all to find

I spoke to the Basket
I asked what it had planned
It Said
"There is Something important
I need you to understand

I represent the world
The food I hold is Gifts and Talents
Everyone has everything
They need
We just need to get in Balance

We are desperate
To be the same
But that won't happen
Don't you see?
That's why we need each other
Diversity is the key

While your gift
May be cooking
And mine is making Tea
When we combine the two
They complement each other perfectly

So never be envious
Of the gifts
Someone else
May have
By combining them
We help each other
And gain Rapport

Now that's got to be fab!!

Claire Bloomfield (25th January 2021)

The Puzzle

I had a realisation
Just the other day
I was Desperate
To explain it
Although I didn't
Know what to say

Now I Know and see
In my mind's eye
The things I didn't understand
It has been something
That made me feel so Grand

I've always valued my Faith
It means so much to me
It is very Special
A Real gift to me

As a child
I knew God as a friend
His friendship meant
So much to me
When others didn't understand
He would look after me

As a teenager
People told me
God loved me

I didn't understand why
I didn't like or love myself
Was my Faith a lie?

My Faith had phases
Went up and down
Like Tower Bridge
I love God
But would get angry
And disown him
When hard things happened
Then I'd hit a ridge

I used to want to sew
But sewing was very hard for me
Using a piece of Binka
Was the only way for me

Binka is material with holes in
From the back
It looks a mess
Unless you look at the front
The end result
You cannot guess

The Binka is a picture
Of the way my life
Appeared to me
Don't miss understand
I was happy

However things happened quite randomly

These were my thoughts
Until quite recently
I undertook a course
Of Neurolinguistic Programming (NLP)
Through studying NLP
I finally understand
That nothing is random
It's all connected and planned

It has challenged my view
And caused me to see
That everything is
Exactly how it should be

NLP Teaches that we all have a world view
The way we understand
Will be different
It's true
It's down to our perception
And the lens we look through
But when it comes to the crunch
We're all the same
We are all connected
We need each other
Understanding and Rapport
Should be our ultimate aim

Claire Bloomfield (3rd February 2021)

'Let your smile change the world but don't let your world change your Smile.'

Chapter Eight

HELPLINE

I became involved in doing voluntary work for Premier Christian Radio. I met Olave, who has subsequently become one of my best friends. Olave was a presenter for Premier.

During my interview for this work, she asked me whether I would be prepared to go on her programme and share my faith. This, I gladly agreed to do. Little did I know at the time that Olave would be the key to my freedom as I was feeling very insecure with low self-esteem. I could not get her out of my mind and began to focus on ways to bless her. I wrote to her the next day and began to pray for her. In subsequent meetings, we would pray for issues, including Olave's sister Judy.

Judy lives in South Africa. She was experiencing difficulties. Our prayers seemed to help as her situation changed. Judy came to London on holiday and asked if she could meet me.

We met and had a great time together. I thought that was the end of our story but that was not so. I was experiencing difficulties in my relationship with my Mum and felt God was telling me that if I shared my anguish with Judy that my emotional pain would be resolved and I would be able to move on. Judy and I met again, during which time I shared my pain with her.

During the evening of the same day, I became very tearful and experienced very bad stomach cramps. On retiring to bed, I had a picture in my mind of a large granite stone in the middle of the living room floor. God told me that it was the pain I had carried with me and that I would not experience it anymore. I was doubtful because I had carried it around for so long. However, the next day it was gone with only emptiness in its place. I wondered why I wasn't elated. I was neither happy nor sad. Then I read Mark 4.35 in the Bible as the daily reading. It detailed when the disciples went across the lake and referred to being neither one side nor the other. It mentioned that often, when a traumatic experience is released that people are often in limbo. When I knew that the way I was feeling was acceptable, I was able to embrace the freedom.

Judy and I became firm friends and she invited me to visit her in South Africa. In the meantime, Olave became ill and I wanted to see her, which meant getting a train, something which I hadn't done on my own before. Now that I had an invite to South Africa and would have to get on a plane on my own, I reasoned that it didn't make sense not to travel on a train. So, I took a train to visit her. As a result of overcoming my fears, I have had the privilege of going to South Africa for a few years running.

In 1999 I at last found the job I have now. It should have been for six weeks but so far has lasted nine years. This is not something I see myself doing forever, but it has given me the confidence to believe I am capable of more.

Another of the biggest influences in my journey has been meeting a lady called Gina, who has been and continues to be a huge support, especially helping me with my bereavement over my Mother. At first, following this event, I believed my life was over. Gina helped me realise that it is just in a different phase. She is one of the inspirations behind my desire to share my journey with others.

Healing

When your Self
Is Fractured
And your Soul
Is Sad
Call the Broken pieces back
Then you'll no longer feel Bad

You have dreams
That lay dormant
That you've shut away
Because you didn't believe
They'd ever see the light of Day

When you are privileged to
Tap into your Subconscious Mind
You can then leave all
Your limitations Behind

Anything can limit you
Including fear, trauma, Pain or hurt
Indeed, Even the journey towards
Freedom can hurt

It's hard – there's a safety
In staying stuck
Where you are
But, it's an illusion
Break it
And you will go far

Break from your Bondage
Then you will see
The world is your Oyster
You will be Free!!

Claire Bloomfield (4th February 2021)

'Your life is 10% what happens to you and 90% what you do about it.'

Charles R Swindoll

Chapter Nine

ADVENTURE

Blazing New Trails

I went on a holiday to South Africa that started to help me get my mind around different things. The first holiday to South Africa was in 2004, and then I went on holiday there for the following twelve years, and I went there every year I met different people. I started by going out there because a friend of mine worked for Premier radio. I was involved with Premier radio, the helpline; I used to be involved with them. My friend and her sister were both South African. She said to me one time that her sister was coming over to England and whether I wanted to meet her so we would go out for lunch.

So, we went out for lunch and on that particular day, she started talking about a house that she was building out in South Africa and she told me that when it was ready I could come over and visit it if I wanted to.

I so wanted to go on holiday. I'd never been farther than Watford and for her to ask really made my day. I loved travelling. I had only gone abroad with my Mum and Dad to Spain which was my first holiday abroad. I didn't like it, it was just way too hot for me and I went once to Holland for a long weekend with another friend of mine and stayed with a mutual friend which was alright. I was 22 when I went abroad with my Mum and Dad.

The trip to South Africa was a solo trip. It was an amazing trip. I loved it. I can still remember everything about it, even on the plane. I couldn't believe that it was actually going to happen because it was so far out of my comfort zone and so alien to me to be truly living a dream.

When Judy invited me, I used to tell people that I was going to South Africa. I kept saying it because the more you say it, the more it becomes real to you. I used to tell people and I used to see them look at me thinking, 'How are you going to do that now? Be realistic!' So I kept saying 'I'm going! I'm going to South Africa, I know I am.'

I had a very good friend at the church and she told me that she would pray for me to go. So, we sat at my kitchen table and we prayed for this holiday to happen. I can remember being on the plane and landing when it was really early in the morning, and I thought, *'Wow!'* I just started crying because it affected me so much to believe that I was actually there; it was an awesome experience.

This particular holiday broke so many of the preconceptions that people had that I couldn't do this or I couldn't do that. You just have to get in your mind that you can do it; it's not about what you can't do but what you can do. As long as you have people who understand you and are willing to help you along the way, then nothing is impossible.

My Dad was very protective; we had a really good friendship as it were. I knew he didn't really want me to go because he'd kept me in a bubble and protected me all this time. It was the fear factor for my parents and wondering if I would be okay alone. He kept wondering, 'What if this happens, what if that happens?' I had to speak up and eventually blurted out to him,

"I was born with a voice I can actually speak to people and nothing is going to happen that I can't control. Judy is going to be there anyway and it's not going to be that bad!"

And it was one of the best things I could have ever done and I will never forget those experiences. I can't see myself going out there again because I have my cats now and I don't see myself leaving my girls behind for two weeks. At the time though it was the most wonderful thing ever.

If people stay in their comfort zones; you won't grow at all. Before that experience, I'd never actually done anything like that before. I remember I wanted to go see a friend of mine because she hadn't been well. This was the same friend who worked for Premier radio. I started speaking to God because I always used to talk to God and ask him what to do. I felt comfortable telling him about my thoughts and asking him for solutions. I started muttering to God, asking,

"How can I go and see her because it's expensive to get a taxi for £70.00 to travel up to London?"

and I heard God reply back to me my mind,

"Well, I'll take you up there."

I've been with my friend to the Premier training before and well I thought I could do this, so I told nobody that I was going and, in my mind, Judy had already invited me to South Africa. I needed to travel to London first before I could attempt any other long-distance travel by myself. I have never travelled by myself, so if I can't do this how will I travel all the way up to South Africa?

So the following day, I got everything organised and got on a train to the station and I can tell you with complete certainty that God actually organised everything, even down to the taxi that I got on. I saw the taxi just across the road to where I wanted to go and I muttered to myself,

"I want that taxi!"

and it just came, and everything about that journey was magical. When I got there, my friend was like,

"What are you doing here?"

so, I said,

"I came to see you and I told nobody because if I told anyone, they would have said don't go because it's far too dangerous."

So, I went on my own to see her, which opened up so much

for me and I did exactly what I wanted to do. I needed to do that because I needed to break the cycle of people thinking that I couldn't do things and that I have a limiting belief that I couldn't do these things. I still felt physically ill when I got there purely because of the stress of how to get there. Going the first time by myself, I realised I could actually go anywhere. It was stressful but I would never ever not do it for the world because I loved it. I had to build up to it and then it was absolutely fine.

The thing is that you should want more of what's on the other side of the fear, then the fear is not going to grab you that much. If you think that's too much and you don't actually want what's on the other side then fear will take over. But as long as you overcome that fear, you can get to your final destination with ease. It's all down to your mindset.

And so, the journey begins. Here I sit, writing my life's journey to you, to give inspiration and hope to those who feel they are stuck or have lost belief in themselves and show you that life can throw multiple challenges at you. Still, it's how you overcome those challenges and keep fighting for what you want that makes the difference. If I can do it, then so can you. With my book, I'm hoping to change as many lives as possible.

YMCA - A Life-Changing Experience

When I first entered the Doors of Romford YMCA, I had no idea that I was starting a journey that would completely change my life and my perception.

Perhaps I should explain, initially, I went to the gym because I wanted to do a sponsored bike ride for a charity in South Africa called Plett Aid Foundation, only one problem - I couldn't ride a bike! However, I remembered from a previous visit that Romford gym had hand bikes. Consequently, I told myself I would just undertake the Sponsorship and leave. Those were my thoughts. However, I was so wrong - I completed the Sponsorship very satisfactorily. The following week I noticed the static cycles and decided that I wanted to ride them. Initially, this felt impossible. However, I achieved this over time, along with the instructors' patience and dedication, literally turning my feet on the pedals. It was a great day when I could do this unaided - another goal reached. I was just using my wheelchair up to this point. Eventually, because a friend offered me a lift to the gym, I finally took my sticks to the gym and started walking. After some time, I wanted to use the treadmill - my friend used it and so I didn't want to be left out. This goal was again only achieved by the patience and dedication of the instructors!

During my time at the YMCA and being a gym instructor, and improving my own fitness, I spent some time assisting the chaplain, which I really enjoyed.

It is not an exaggeration to say that attending the gym has saved my life both personally and emotionally. Being part of the Instruct Ability Programme means the world to me - I have an opportunity to be an ambassador both for Romford YMCA and Instruct Ability. I never imagined that I could be where I am now - on the way to becoming an instructor - EEK!!! WOW!!!

Firewalk – An Unforgettable Mind-Blowing Experience

Firewalking – a new lease of life's blazing trials. The whole experience was unforgettable. I didn't let my disability stop me. I used to be a part of the YES group. Mostly for people within a business. They did basket brigades where you make baskets with bits of food for Christmas etc. They had speakers come in every fortnight and speak about their own brand of their business. This particular time they said they were going to do this firewalk. My friend wanted to do it. It's absolutely crazy,] but I was so intrigued. I actually thought to myself, 'Wow, I'm going to do a firewalk!' I didn't tell anyone that I was going to do it because I thought no one would want to sponsor me, especially if I don't have any physical balance.

The thought of me walking across on a pile of coal just felt and sounded so ludicrous but I just had to do it. I was going to do it because I felt like it. I knew I was going to love the challenge. We got signed up for it. When we arrived there, the group leader had already been in touch with the coordinators and confirmed that we could do it. First, we had to go into a room and as we walked in, I saw a gentleman standing in the middle. I did not know why this chap was jumping up and down in the middle of the room. So, I thought I'd just follow his lead and get involved with the music. We were supposed to be practising going barefoot across the room. We were literally mimicking exactly how a firewalk would be like. The energy in the room lit up and I was so ready to go.

We walked outside to do this and I kept telling myself no one is going to stop me from doing this, absolutely no one.
The overriding thing was the madness in the room that day; the music was so loud and the gentleman running the event was jumping up and down, boosting up everyone's energy levels. I thought he had completely lost it but I understood why he was going that later on; it was to enable us to get into the right state of mind.

I just followed the instructions and was so determined to do this and prove anybody that thought I couldn't do it wrong but more for me to prove that I'm capable of doing anything that I put my mind to.

Even in the middle of the firewalk, I actually stopped as I thought it wasn't that hot. It doesn't look that dangerous when I physically looked at the ashes laid out in a line on the grass.

We were the last ones to complete the firewalk, my friend and I, due to insurance purposes, weren't allowed to go first. Tosin (the gentleman who was jumping up and down in the middle of the room) and Steve (who assisted) helped me to cross the fire and when I stopped midway, I could hear them screaming,

"Don't stop in the middle, it will burn your feet! Keep going!"

I actually stopped for a few seconds just to prove to myself that there was actually ash there. It just felt so unreal. When you've completed a life-changing experience like this, the adrenaline rush from actually completing it felt like I couldn't come down from it for ages. I was so proud of myself for achieving what I set out to do. The thing about fear is that it gets in your mind in a loop and goes around and around, whittling away at you until you overcome the fear and experience the joy. It was pretty surreal. The walk across the coal was over in seconds. The build-up took thirty minutes and in less than five, the fear was taken away!

The main tip was that if you overthink things, then it won't work. You have to keep your focus on the end goal and just go for it. The core of it being mind over matter, I had to ignore the fact that it was hot. My focus had to be on the end result of walking over the ashes and onto the grass to wipe my feet. If you can control your mind to think you can do it and to not focus on it being hard, then it can be accomplished.

At first glance, what might have seemed scary is actually a spectacular occurrence to watch (and to experience firsthand, as I recently discovered) as individuals walked over the fire that generated a deeper, fresher attitude.

In all things, there are inherent dangers. You can end up with a slight blister while fire walking or end up being burnt. It's all about your confidence that when you go through it, what's going to happen will happen. The only reason you think, at first that anything like this is not possible is because you were conditioned with this conviction as a child. You were told somewhere along the way, *"Don't touch that; it's hot."* The belief is something you have been programmed to believe—just step beyond the belief and then anything's possible.

Hot Air Balloon Ride

My friend from the YMCA (Young Men's Christians

Association) was doing the hot air balloon ride. She mentioned to me that she was doing it, so I asked her whether I would be able to do it too, and she said,

"Yes, probably can as long as you can stand in the balloon."

So, I rang up Virgin Balloons on the same day and explained to them my situation, that I do have a disability and that I can't stand for long periods but I am able to stand and whether they think that I would be alright to undertake the activity. They said yes, as long as I could stand and hold on, it would be fine. Nothing was stopping me from going into the balloon.

This took place in 2017 and there was a long wait before we could do the hot air balloon experience and I'm still waiting to get up a second time.

The thing was, I'm not fond of heights very much, so I wondered whether I could manage it. However, when I saw the balloon, it had a basket at the bottom which was all closed in, so it looked safe and secure and there was no fear of you falling out, which gave me the confidence that it would be alright. Once I realised that it was game on, I knew I could do it as there was no danger involved. It was sectioned off so that you can go with people you're with. It was an amazing experience.

Before getting into the balloon, they explained how to get in and out and when we would go up in the air, a couple of minutes later, they said,

"Do you want to get into the landing position?"

and I was like,

"Already, we've only just got up here."

And he said,

"No, we've been up here for just over an hour now; we have got to go back."

I was thinking, 'Do we have to?' It was just such a surreal experience. It was a different world up there. Everything looked so small and you could wave to people. It was so peaceful. It was a dream come true for me. Never in a million years did I think I would be able to stand for that long in a hot air balloon.

NLP

NLP relies on the subconscious mind. With the specific HYET method of healing your emotional trail taught through the NLP course. We first learned to gain rapport with our clients, which means getting to know what they are doing in life. So, you have to do the same dance together. For example, you have silhouette people. You can't do your own dance while the other person is doing something else, so you have to do the same thing they are doing. You would ask them what sort of emotions they were looking to lose and gain rapport with them. You could be dealing with feelings of anger, sadness, fear, guilt or shame.
I love this quote that I saw by Nicky Gumbel:

"We may impress people with our strengths, but we connect with people through our Vulnerabilities."

I think I have been aware of this for ages but connected with it recently - a real light bulb moment.
I used to be very afraid of showing weakness but now realise that it is actually a strength! I always thought it was necessary to cope all the time and although it is good to manage, rapport comes with connection.

The Lightbulb Experience

Today I had an experience
Which felt really unreal
I know it will bring me more freedom
I need to process it
However, it is giving me the
Urge to jump up and down
That's right now
How I feel

I am being vague I know
So please bear with me
Then the reason
For my Elation
I'm hoping you will see

All my life
I've been taught to believe
That to show strength was vital
That you should never
Ask to receive help
As then you will appear weak
You need to be strong
To cope at all times
So to speak

Over time through my Faith
I learnt to see
That being Strong
Wasn't all it was

Cracked up to be
In some situations
I needed
To show how I felt
If I Couldn't a more serious
Blow could be dealt

Thankfully now
I'm more able to express
How I feel
I have discovered
That I won't die
If I'm real.

In fact, far from being a weakness
The opposite is true
Being real and transparent
Will bring freedom to you

Being real doesn't mean
You're weak
Or can't cope
No not at all
It just means
You will build Rapport and unity with others
That's all
Which will ultimately
Give you more strength
To stand Tall

Claire Bloomfield (19th February 2021)

'We are all Visitors to Earth - our Purpose is to observe, to Learn, to grow, and to Love.'

Australian Aborigines

Chapter Ten

OPPORTUNITY

What Next?

You've done amazing things; what next now. Coaching, mastering skill set and helping others. Book to gain clients and inspire others and coach them.

I wanted to be able to coach people and give them the tools to help themselves. I've realised that everything is so connected. When you realise nothing is random, as I used to think things were, it's amazing. Nothing is a coincidence. It's the energy you drive towards yourself. With the actions you take and with the correct mindset, you can achieve anything you put your mind and soul into.

I've come to realise that by knowing that you can do anything that you set your mind to; anything is possible— you are not limited by my own thoughts. You still have restrictions, sure. I just don't want to feel like I'm going all over the place, but I would like to do conferences on my journey and make people aware that they can get the freedom I had; if they want it, that is. I've always known but it has come to me quite forcefully in the last couple of days that you can't sit still if you want change. If you wish to change, you've got to drive it. It's not going to fall into your lap. If I hadn't taken the initiative and put my foot forward and have been willing to come out of my comfort zone to explore the possibilities I had, I couldn't have sat here today writing down my life journey for you.

The opportunities are there as well as the signposts. But unless you move and take action, then nothing is going to change.

YOU HAVE TO TAKE ACTION.

·I've got a friend who, to be fair she kind of says a lot of things and says this, that and the other but she waits for things to fall into her lap and I sit there thinking why don't you just do it if you want to do it.

I'm intolerant as I can see things and think, 'Why didn't you go after it?' However, earlier on in my life, I was a bit like that. You want to be included in the bubble. If other people do it, you don't have to take responsibility. At the end of the day, if you want change, that's the only way it's going to go.

As a qualified NLP coach, I am able to teach others on the expertise I have learnt throughout my life.

In the last couple of days, there have been light bulb moments for me. My journey towards freedom, as I realised, was that I could be free with or without my disability. The disability doesn't have any bearing as to whether I'm free or not. It's a casing; it doesn't control me. I can still be free and not let it overtake me. You need to be physically and emotionally strong.

Are you ready to take your life into your own hands and take action?

I sure was!

Believe in yourself, and anything is possible!

Dreams

My future dreams and things I hope to accomplish is board breaking and to get driven around in a racing car. I love the need for speed. I would also like to do another hot air balloon ride as it was such a surreal experience the first time around. I just want to do it again in my lifetime.

Let's make our dreams come true and live a life of fulfillment.

It definitely was my turn and I'm proud of my journey and the person I've become on my road to freedom!

Poem Lockdown Life

At first when lockdown hit
It really freaked me out
Three weeks without seeing friends??
Or in fact… wait for it…
Leaving my home at all!!
Oh dear Boris
You can't be serious
What is it all about

In my panic
I contacted a good friend
I asked how can this be right or true
She sent me a beautiful piece of music
It said "God is with us"
Don't worry he is in the storm with you

You know the thing is
I discovered over time
My friend Was/ is right
At first this whole situation
Felt impossible
I wanted to leave
To take flight

But now
There is a rhythm
There is a pace
Although I haven't through choice
Ventured out much

I have enjoyed catching up on Zoom
Had the occasional cuppa with friends
Seen a few people face-to-face
Done jigsaws on my iPad
Learned French through Duolingo too
Even managed to catch up on my soaps on TV
Goodness I've seen home and away right the way through
I'm also a cat mum
I love being with my girls
So yes I can say with confidence
That although lockdown is not easy
The time has given me some pearls

My biggest lesson has been
That when we change our mind
Through God's Grace
The Blessings far outweigh
The struggles we are called to Face

Claire Bloomfield

'Let your light shine brightly so others can find their way out of the dark.'

Maya Angelou

I now have the privilege of living in my family home, which I moved back into on 27th July 2015 (My Dad's birthday). Cassie is one of three rescue cats who shares my house and turns it from a house into a home. My other cats are Sophie and Bella. They are my world.

The Question / Paradox

What's your situation?
Where are you at right now
Is life a bed of Roses
Or an extremely painful Ouch

Whatever situation you're in
Whatever your current lot may be
You know you do have choices
You can stay there, move or be free

You can stay in your resentment
Wallowing on the couch
That is allowed for a season
However, it will only
Increase your pain
Added to that
You could be a grouch
Then there is nothing to gain

However, I recently discovered
That everyone is on their own personal journey
Sometimes there are miracles
Which are lovely to see
And yes sometimes we have to go through
To be free

Sometimes nothing changes
At least physically

Nothing at all
But even at those times
It's still possible to have a ball

It's difficult to understand
That even in hard situations
We can retain our inner Glow
It's in embracing our challenges
And using them as our energy
That's when we grow

This is a work in progress for me
Honestly, I never thought
I could embrace my disability
That in no way means
I'm controlled by it
And I can never improve
However, in embracing everything
That makes me
Who I am while looking above
I can go forward
With a heart
Filled with gratitude Peace and love

Claire Bloomfield (6th March 2021)

*'Never be ashamed or afraid of your mess;
you wouldn't have a message without a
mess.'*

ACKNOWLEDGEMENTS

I would like to thank Tosin,
Lorna and Labosshy (Labs) without
whom this book would have
remained a figment of my imagination.
Thank you all for being part of
bringing it to life.
You are all very special indeed.

.

'It always seems impossible until it's done.'

Nelson Mandela

Printed in Great Britain
by Amazon